WHO SHOT ESTEVAN LIGHT?

Caitlin Press Inc.
3375 Ponderosa Way
Qualicum Beach, BC V9K 2J8
www.caitlinpress.com

Text and cover design by Vici Johnstone
Cover image: Estevan Lighthouse. Image credit: Living Cowichan via Wikimedia Commons, public domain.

Printed in Canada

Caitlin Press Inc. acknowledges financial support from the Government of Canada and the Canada Council for the Arts, and the Province of British Columbia through the British Columbia Arts Council and the Book Publisher's Tax Credit.

Who shot Estevan Light? : and other tales from the Salish Sea and beyond / Douglas Hamilton.
Hamilton, Douglas L., 1945- author
Canadiana 20240447867 | ISBN 9781773861531 (softcover)
LCSH: Navigation—British Columbia—History—Anecdotes | LCSH: British Columbia—History—
   Anecdotes.
LCC FC3811 .H36 2024 | DDC 971.1—dc23

Who Shot Estevan Light?

*And Other Tales from the
Salish Sea and Beyond*

Douglas Hamilton

Caitlin Press

*For my life partner Penny Sadler without whose help,
editorial and otherwise, this book would not have been possible.*

Contents

PART 3

EXPEDITIONS

PART 4

LASQUETI CHARACTERS OF THE 1970s

Part 1

EARLY HISTORY:
TALES FROM AN ENCHANTED ISLAND

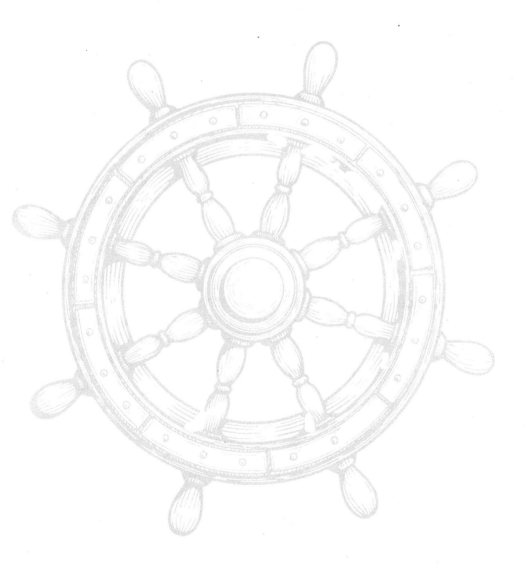

THE LEGEND OF THE
FLYING DUTCHMAN

I have long been fascinated by the malfeasance of those policemen who betray the public trust. This story came to me in many layers, from the Provincial Police magazine, *The Shoulder Strap*, files at BC archives, local newspapers of the day, and finally a chat with Cecil (Nobby) Clark, author of *Tales of the British Columbia Provincial Police*. Although a true believer at the start of the process, I discovered the story of the connection between the Cassidy Gang and the Dutchman to be a gross fabrication.

In the early years of the 20th century Henry Wagner, also known as the Flying Dutchman, used a fast twin-engine motorboat to smuggle, pillage and steal along the inner coast from Seattle to Comox. Between 1911 and 1913 he and his accomplice, Bill Julian, based their nefarious activities on remote Lasqueti Island, perfectly situated for expeditions to the prosperous coal-mining communities of Nanaimo, Wellington and Union Bay on Vancouver Island.

On the eve of the First World War, Union Bay was one of the largest towns in BC with a population of more than thirteen thousand. The Fraser Bishop Store was the largest retail establishment north of Victoria and it lay only 100 metres from the beach. Such easy access was a powerful temptation to water-borne buccaneers. To stop the repeated break-ins, Chief Constable David T. Stevenson of the BC Provincial Police (BCPP) decided to lay a trap for the thieves. He appointed two burly constables, Gordon Ross and Harry Westaway, to pose as job hunters in the town. They were told to keep a low profile and patrol around the store at night.

At around 3:00 a.m. on a rainy March 3, 1913, their vigilance was rewarded. A flickering light was seen in the darkened store. The officers drew their revolvers and entered, surprising two burglars who were also armed with at least one Colt pistol. In a fierce struggle, all lights were extinguished, several shots sounded, and Constable Westaway fell mortally wounded with a bullet through the chest. One thief fled while Ross took on the other in an epic battle involving pistol butts, billy clubs and fists. At the end both men were almost unrecognizable, and the store was half demolished, but the intruder lay senseless at Ross's feet.

With a policeman dead and a suspect in custody, Chief Constable Stevenson hurried from Nanaimo to interview the prisoner. A large mole on the right cheek soon revealed his true identity. It was "Jack the Flying Dutchman" a.k.a. Henry Wagner, a smuggler and pirate well known to American lawmen in Puget Sound. His accomplice, Bill Julian, was nabbed a few days later on Lasqueti Island. Sharp-eyed Constable George Hannay remembered seeing the two men living on a small homestead on the north end of Lasqueti.

Henry Wagner, a notorious BC pirate based on Lasqueti Island. With a faster boat than the police, he eluded capture for years and was reputed to be part of Butch Cassidy's gang. Image credit: I1-163 Nanaimo Museum

During the trial in Nanaimo, Wagner was the subject of much public attention throughout the Northwest. The *Nanaimo Free Press* described him as about thirty-nine years old, bowlegged and 170 pounds, with stooping shoulders. The report went on to say, "he possesses a broad and expansive forehead denoting great intelligence which evidently has been cultivated in the wrong direction. His worst feature is his eyes which are steely blue, cold, callous and unimpressionable; although his movements are slow and stealthy, his gift of calculation is keenly developed." American authorities were so concerned that they sent an officer to the trial to re-arrest the Dutchman for crimes committed south of the border if he should somehow beat the murder rap.

Bill Julian, his accomplice, testified enthusiastically against his former partner. He professed a terrible fear of Wagner and gave evidence that implicated him in dozens of armed robberies using the speedy motorboat. Wagner followed "…every movement of Julian in court with hypnotic vindictiveness." The death of Constable Westaway proved decisive.

Julian received only five years as a reward for his testimony while Henry Wagner was sentenced to death by hanging for murder.

The Dutchman swore he would never hang and made a determined effort at suicide by bashing his head against the iron bars of his cell when the attention of his guard was elsewhere. He was double shackled, and another guard was placed in the cell for the remainder of his stay.

Justice was speedy. On the morning of August 28, 1913, the Salvation Army chaplain visited the condemned man. Wagner apologized for his life of crime, noting that the loss of his mother at an early age had deprived him of direction at a critical juncture in his life—an interesting Freudian insight. He asked the chaplain to preach a sermon on the dangers of evil companions. His last words were, "Remember me to my wife, though she had a dark skin, her heart was white."

At this time, the Nanaimo Jail was packed with hundreds of coal miners imprisoned for their role in the Great Vancouver Island Coal Strike of August 1913. As Wagner was led to the gallows, fellow prisoners sent him on his way with a sad wailing dirge. It is not hard to imagine what they thought of the "King's Justice." The execution was all over in forty seconds. "…his passing was carried out with such precision that a new world's record was established in executions of that type…" enthused one local paper. And so the story rested for twenty-six years. Then in 1939, things took a new and bizarre turn. *The Shoulder Strap* magazine, the chief propaganda organ of the BC Provincial Police, ran a story by A.J. McKelvie that made startling claims, which have since become enshrined in the legend of the Flying Dutchman. In a long six-page article McKelvie observed:

> Who among western officers had not heard of Henry Wagner, alias Henry Ferguson and a dozen other aliases, and notoriously known as the "Flying Dutchman?" He was an almost mythical figure representing the last and worst of the bad men of the Old West.
>
> Some years previous he had been chief of the infamous Cassidy Gang, which had terrorized Wyoming and neighbouring states, a gang that had committed scores of murders, hold-ups and train robberies. Sheriff's posses had failed to round up this vicious gang and eventually Uncle Sam sent out his hard-riding cavalry with orders to exterminate these 'human rats.' The soldiers did their work well. Eighteen of the outlaws were shot down, but the "Flying Dutchman" and his henchman, Bill, sought safety in flight.

Wagner and Bill continued their criminal careers and staged many robberies and burglaries. They served prison terms and, in some instances, escaped from custody. Each time their connection with the Cassidy gang was not established until after they were free. Attempting to rob a post office in the State of Washington, Wagner shot and killed the postmaster. He and his evil aide then completely disappeared, only to appear at Union Bay and add another murder to their long list of similar crimes.

What a capture for a "rookie cop"! This whimsical rewriting of history quickly took on a life of its own and is accepted as fact today. Indeed, every story about the Flying Dutchman that has appeared since then dwells at length on the Butch Cassidy connection. But does it hold up under close scrutiny?

During the trial in 1913, newspapers all over the Northwest carried the story of Wagner's epic struggle with Constable Ross, and his arrest at Union Bay. They also detailed his past history and criminal exploits. But there was not a word about any Butch Cassidy connection. Surely such an association would have been a huge story in 1913 when the notorious gang was world famous.

The Hole-in-the-Wall Gang's hideout in Johnson County, Wyoming, was never successfully penetrated by lawmen, and there were never "eighteen of the outlaws... shot down" in a big shootout with US soldiers. As far as is known, none of the principal gang members ever visited Canada, and none bore the name of Henry Wagner, Henry Ferguson or the Flying Dutchman. For the record, their names were Butch Cassidy, the Sundance Kid, Kid Curry, Lonnie Curry, Laughing Sam Carey, Black Jack Ketchum, Elzy Lay and George Flat Nose Curry.

In 1989 I had the opportunity to chat with Cecil (Nobby) Clark, author of *Tales of the British Columbia Provincial Police*. Clark joined the Provincial Police in 1917, and was in his mid-nineties when I interviewed him in a retirement home in Victoria. He had written about the Dutchman in his book, and had repeated the Butch Cassidy story. Yes, Clark said, he remembered the case well and had actually met Bill Julian in 1919 in Rivers Inlet where Clark was working as a cook. When I asked him about the Butch Cassidy/Henry Wagner connection, he gently smiled and declined comment. That really clinched it. There is simply not a shred of evidence that Henry Wagner was in any way ever associated with Butch Cassidy and the Wyoming Hole-in-the-Wall Gang.

According to the newspapers of the time, Henry Wagner was born in Louisiana in the 1870s. It was believed he spent his early life as a locksmith, and was known to have a way with machinery and boats. He arrived in the Northwest in the early 1890s, and remained there for the rest of his short turbulent life. Dabbling in a variety of illegal enterprises, he was a true career criminal. Smuggling was particularly profitable in the late 19th century. Chinese workers had been forbidden entrance to the US since the Chinese Exclusion Act of 1882. Hopeful immigrants sailed instead to Victoria, and then paid $100 a head to be secretly landed in Washington State. Also popular were opium and Chinese wine—both illegal in the States. Wool was worth 22 cents more south of the border if duties could be avoided. Canadian whiskey was also a good seller, especially in Indigenous villages where it was technically forbidden on both sides of the line. Wagner was a consummate smuggler taking up whatever was most profitable at the time—be it people, booze or items with high duty. He cultivated close friendships with tribal groups, using their remote locations as a base for his activities. They often sheltered him, and eventually he married an Indigenous woman.

The Dutchman befriended a French Canadian named Bill Julian, and together they became a two-man crime wave, stealing from fish traps, stores, warehouses, docks and boats. In 1901 their luck ran out, and they were cornered on tiny Skagit Island in Puget Sound. The pair was captured after a brief shootout and Wagner was sentenced to fourteen years at Walla Walla Penitentiary. He was released early for good behaviour in 1908 and quickly resumed his old partnership with Julian.

This time they procured the *Spray*, a powerful twin-engine motorboat, one of the first to appear on the coast. Probably built in Puget Sound for the smuggling trade, the *Spray* was cutting-edge technology for the day. At 30 feet long and narrow in the beam, it could make over 20 knots. With the *Spray*, they began to raid coastal post offices at Whidbey Island, Bremerton and Langley, Washington, looking for payroll and valuables. They proved impossible to catch thanks to their swift boat and help from local First Nations. In 1912, the Washington Legislature placed a $200 price on Wagner's head.

Clearly it was getting time to move on, so the pair decided to settle on remote Lasqueti Island. The island had a population of less than a hundred at the time, and Wagner brought along his pregnant wife, two young children, a number of small boats and the infamous *Spray*. Residents remember the boat because of its twin screws, which was highly unusual for the time. The Dutchman and Julian fitted right into the small community, even attending a meeting of the Farmers Institute on the night of the

Union Bay robbery. Locals were shocked and stunned by the events that followed. The Flying Dutchman demonstrated an unusual appreciation for the rapidly changing technologies of the early 20th century. In addition to piloting the fastest boat in the area, he showed great ingenuity in adapting other inventions to a life of crime. After his arrest in Union Bay, police discovered a cunning electric light consisting of dry cell batteries for his pocket with wires to a small bulb to be cupped in the hand. Old-timers on Lasqueti tell of a wooden track leading up from the beach into the woods. When the police got close, the boat simply vanished from the bay into a hidden shed. And *Spray* was rendered practically noiseless by an elaborate arrangement of piping that appeared to be a normal exhaust.

A question lingers. What could have possessed *The Shoulder Strap* and BC Provincial Police to concoct this phoney Butch Cassidy story? We can only speculate, but the answer probably lies in the dynamics of changing police jurisdiction in Canada between the wars. By the 1930s the BC Provincial Police realized that the greatest threat to its existence came not from crime but from its archrival, the federal Royal Canadian Mounted Police. During those years three prairie and three maritime provinces replaced their provincial forces with the men in scarlet. *The Shoulder Strap* ran as a quarterly between 1938 and the mid-1950s, and it appealed to the public's love of good action stories, while also touting the force's many genuine accomplishments. Honking a loud horn meant survival in the dirty thirties both for the Provincial Police and their magazine. How tempting and easy it must have been to stretch the truth for a good story.

So what are we to make of the Flying Dutchman? He was certainly a most rapacious, intelligent and aggressive thief. But was he the cold-blooded multiple murderer the Provincial Police claimed? The *Victoria Daily Colonist* observed the day after his arrest in 1913: "Ferguson has served time in Walla Walla Penitentiary, and is a desperate man who, the police have predicted, would end by committing murder." In other words, he had no record of murder before his arrest in Union Bay. It is even possible, though unlikely, that Constable Westaway's death was a ghastly mistake committed during the mad shootout in the darkened store. As the defence had argued during the trial, with all that gunplay either side could have shot the policeman. But an officer of the law had been killed during a felony. The price in those days was death by hanging no matter who pulled the trigger. So ended the sad, later grossly inflated story of Henry Wagner, Lasqueti Island's most famous criminal.

EARLY SPANISH FOOTPRINTS IN BC

Antique maps and what they tell us about the past representations of lands in the rest of the world are fascinating. They present mysteries that call out for solving. A good example is California Island, which appeared in early maps of the California coast (see opposite page). Although this is pure speculation on my part this map (and others) looks a lot like Vancouver Island.

The great 18th-century explorations of the Pacific Northwest by James Cook, George Vancouver, La Pérouse and others have long excited admiration and fascination. These daring voyages were skilfully led, well organized and financed and, above all, well publicized through the explorers' lavishly illustrated personal accounts issued soon after the fact. Today, we regard these men as the true Europeans of the Northwest coast. But were they really the first?

Some have claimed that Juan de Fuca, a Greek-born pilot in Spanish service, explored the West Coast of California in 1592. At about the present latitude of the Strait of Juan de Fuca, he reported entering a large inlet. There he sailed around a large inland sea for twenty days, finding many people and lands rich in gold, silver and pearls. Over the years, his claims have had many doubters.

But a curious piece of evidence, until recently overlooked, raises interesting questions about which Europeans were really the first to visit the fog-shrouded shores of BC. In 1625 the Englishman Samuel Purchas published a collection of travel accounts in *Hakluytus Posthumus* or *Purchas his Pilgrimes*. One of these included an essay by Henry Briggs entitled "Treatise of the North-West Passage to the South Sea," with a map of North America. Among the many novel features of this map was the first appearance of the name "Hudson's Bay." But what was really unusual was the depiction of California as a huge island stretching from Baja Mexico to Cape Blanco. This new map created one of cartography's great mysteries, which has remained unsolved to this day. What could have inspired such a strange delusion and why did it persist for so long? Is it possible that "California Island" was really an early rendering of Vancouver Island? No one can say with certainty, but there are a number of reasons to think this might be so.

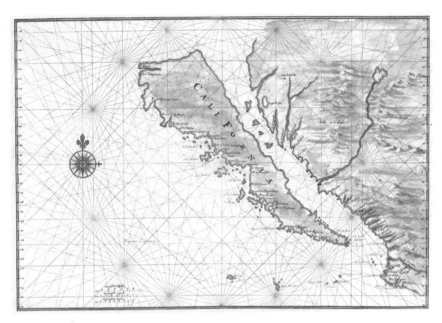

A map of "California Island" created circa 1650, at a time when maps were state secrets or deliberate deceptions. Image credit: Library of Congress via Wikimedia Commons, public domain

For almost two hundred years, California was depicted as an island by most European mapmakers (although doubts were soon raised as to the accuracy of this depiction). What could have inspired such a strange delusion and why did it persist for so long? Is it possible that "California Island" was really an early rendering of Vancouver Island? No one can say with certainty, but there are several reasons to think this might be so. The outline in Briggs's rendering seems strikingly similar to our own coastline. The north-south pitch of California Island approximates that of Vancouver Island, as does the ratio of width to length. Large indentations appear in the central shoreline, and islands dot the inner and outer coast. Fjord-like inlets cut deeply into the mainland across from the island. But there are inconsistencies as well. California Island is shown at least twice the size of Vancouver Island. Furthermore, it lies a thousand miles south of BC. However, mapping was fraught with error in the early 17th century. Latitude was easily determined by measuring the vertical angle of the polar star or the noon sun. But fixing longitude demanded very accurate time measurement over long periods. Inaccurate longitude measurements caused many large continents, oceans and islands to assume bizarre shapes in maps from the 15th to 18th centuries. These strange distortions contribute greatly to the charm of these antique maps.

·Intriguingly, the Briggs map states: "California is sometimes supposed to be part of ye westerne continent but since by a Spanish Charte taken by ye Hollander it is found to be a goodly Illande." Spain, England and Holland at that time were engaged in a series of brutal wars inflamed by religious differences and commercial rivalry. The Briggs map was clearly captured as a prize of war in the early 1600s. Ships' papers and charts were apparently not destroyed in time to prevent them from falling into enemy hands. When questioned, the captured Spanish captain and crew would most likely have refused to explain the large mysterious island off North America that appeared on one of their charts.

Dutch and English mapmakers like Briggs later saw this map (or copies) and hurriedly tried to incorporate the large island into their latest creations. Certainly, if any Spanish captain did sight a large island mass in the eastern Pacific, it could only have been Vancouver Island (or possibly, Haida Gwaii). There are no other islands of substantial size between Alaska and Tierra del Fuego.

With the superb charts and precise satellite-based navigation we enjoy today, it is hard to imagine how different things were in the early 17th century. Spain regarded her nautical charts as highly classified state secrets, and for good reason. These charts often showed the ports and routes used by Spain's treasure ships, which each season moved millions of ounces of silver across the Pacific and Atlantic Oceans from the New World.

With the establishment of a Spanish colony in the Philippines in 1574, a lively trade soon developed on Pacific routes. Silver was shipped from Acapulco to Manila, where it was traded for silk, spices and Chinese porcelain. These products were then sold in Mexico or shipped back to Spain via Panama, thereby avoiding a voyage clear around the world with the risk of encountering Dutch warships near their East Indies strongholds. With such valuable cargoes being transported, it's not surprising that "betraying" charts and other navigational information to Spain's enemies was a crime punishable by death. Even the private printing of maps was discouraged. While exuberant map-makers in Amsterdam, Antwerp, Venice and London filled their atlases with ornate and beautiful works of art, almost nothing survives from Spanish sources, a grand irony considering its great achievements in exploration.

Spain's Pacific trade routes were not without their hazards. Wind patterns, in particular, made travel difficult. On the south-bound leg, easterly trade winds blow in fairly narrow corridors on either side of the equator. Sailors who found the trades could look forward to steady 15–20-knot following breezes with fair weather all the way. Passage from Acapulco to Manila generally took eight to ten weeks on this southerly route. However, the return voyage was very different. Along the equator lay the doldrums, to be avoided at all costs. The Manila galleons were forced into the north Pacific where winds were strong but often unfavourable. This trip could drag on for a gruelling four to seven months, one of the longest sea voyages of the age.

Just how far north the galleons actually sailed is the key question. It's difficult to answer because of Spanish secrecy about their sea routes. But the farther north these ships ventured, the more likely they were to make landfall in the Pacific Northwest. Reports have the returning Manila convoys usually arriving between Cape Mendocino and Baja. However, the winds of the north Pacific would have allowed sailing vessels to track very far north, increasing the duration of a crossing. Difficult sea conditions or fear of enemy privateers would likely have encouraged Spanish captains occasionally to venture farther north than usual. It does not seem unreasonable that during all those years of regular convoy traffic (1590–1812), one or more European ships might have stumbled onto our shores before Cook's arrival. Off the North American coast anywhere from Alaska south, the prevailing summer Pacific high would have provided strong northwesterlies and an easy ride south to Mexico.

It would have been very unusual if Spain did not carry out at least a rudimentary exploration of the Pacific Northwest coastline. Those tons of silver so ruthlessly extracted from Peru and Mexico, and the returning goods from the exotic East were essential for maintaining Spain's place in the world. The vulnerable northern return route could only be used with any degree of safety if it was charted. This need not have involved settlement, just a rough knowledge of the shoreline to avoid hazards and in case of emergency.

So, what do historians have to say about the California Island delusion? Henry Raup Wagner, founder of the California Historical Society and the Northwest coast's premier cartographer, felt it was all an honest mistake on the part of the Spaniards. He believes that Father Fray Antonio de la Ascension, who accompanied the Sebastian Vizcaino expedition to Cape Mendocino in 1603, simply misread the coast. Just before the ships turned back, the Catholic father thought he saw the coastline turn sharply eastward. He assumed California must be an island. Serious exploration then supposedly ceased for almost two hundred years. But the historical record shows that the northern Gulf of California had already been extensively explored by Hernando de Alarcon in 1540, more than sixty years earlier. Maps copied from his originals (now lost) clearly show a peninsula and not an island. Wagner argued that some of Alarcon's key findings were lost or ignored after his return. Yet the idea that Imperial Spain could "forget" about such essential geography does not seem credible, given the enormous sums in silver and other luxury goods that passed along the California coast each year. The myth of California Island took a long time to die. For many years the area remained a backwater with few people of any race, a scattering of Catholic Spanish missions, and no obvious precious metals.

The eastern Pacific remained one of the most isolated places on earth until the 19th century. Because there were so few visitors, many of the great European mapmakers remained uncertain on the island question and resorted to a number of ploys to hide their ignorance. Unknown lands were often covered with ornamentation, illustrations or text. In some atlases, California was shown as an island on one map and part of the mainland on another. It finally fell to the Jesuit priest Eusebio Francisco Kino to settle the matter. Kino, a mathematician and astronomer, arrived in Mexico in 1681 and began a systematic exploration along the Gulf of California for the establishment of missions. In 1705, his findings and a map were published, which once again showed that the Sea of Cortes did not continue northward to make California an island. Tellingly though, it was not until 1747 that Spanish authorities publicly declared California Island to be a geographical error.

Perhaps this should not be surprising. For years, a huge island had appeared in an impossible place on maps of the West Coast. What better way to confuse and mislead Spain's enemies in the Pacific? The whole thing may not have been part of a Spanish "misinformation" campaign, but colonial authorities may well have welcomed the deception created by such a mistake.

Anyone looking for conclusive proof that Spanish galleons were sailing past Vancouver Island around 1600 will be disappointed. Physical evidence, if any existed, is likely long gone. The visits would have been brief and unobtrusive. But in all probability, the Manila convoys had some passing knowledge of BC's coastline, at least extending south from the northern tip of Vancouver Island. The peculiar assumption that Captain Cook was the first "modern" European to happen upon the west coast will eventually have to be re-examined.

LA PÉROUSE, BC's FORGOTTEN EXPLORER

> La Pérouse stands as one of the great explorers of the 18th century. His mapping of the Pacific Northwest can only be compared to the explorations of Captain Cook. The fact that he was French and didn't make it back to civilization meant that his story was almost unknown. What I wouldn't give to know what really happened to his expedition that caused its failure.

Does the name Jean-François de Galaup, comte de La Pérouse ring a bell? If it doesn't maybe it should. Excepting Captain James Cook and his magnificent voyages, La Pérouse was probably the greatest 18th-century European explorer of the wide Pacific. Strangely, he is almost unknown in North America. He even passed briefly through the northwest coast, being among the first to chart the northern coast of British Columbia. Tragically, the expedition ended in disaster on a small island in the Pacific.

In 1785, barely four years before the French Revolution, the French king, Louis XVI, turned his attention to the unexplored reaches of the Pacific Ocean. He felt the Cook expeditions had barely scratched the surface and much remained to be discovered. This new expedition was to demonstrate the glory of France to the world, but commercial and trading possibilities were not to be ignored. Above all, it was to be a scientific effort, involving the best minds and most up-to-date equipment available. In accordance with the ideals of the Age of Enlightenment, there would be no attempt to impose French authority or the Christian religion on Indigenous Peoples. They were to be respected and treated fairly at all times.

In the summer of 1785, two transports were armed as frigates in the port of Brest, rechristened *Boussole* and *Astrolabe*, and placed under the command of La Pérouse. Many of France's most respected scientists, military officers, artists and cartographers vied for the opportunity to accompany the expedition. Newly improved chronometers, essential for determining exact longitude, were also provided. No cost was spared. Curiously, one of the eager applicants was a young Corsican artillery officer by the name of Napoleon Bonaparte. He failed to make the grade, but went on to world-changing things nonetheless.

Jean-François de Galaup, comte de La Pérouse, an undeservedly little-known French explorer who rivalled Captain Cook in the extent of his travels. Image credit: 2Y59F1F Alamy

After rounding Cape Horn, the two ships made brief stops at Chile, Easter Island and Maui before setting course for Alaska. They arrived off the St. Elias mountain range on June 23 and turned south seeking a sheltered bay for a badly needed refit. La Pérouse chose Lituya Bay, and here occurred the first of many misfortunes that were to dog the expedition. Initially all went well, although the Indigenous People, fascinated by the European weapons and clothing, had to be closely watched. Two longboats were taking soundings in the bay when suddenly one was seized by a powerful tidal current and dragged toward a bar at the mouth of the harbour. The men pulled for their lives to escape the savage breakers, but it was no use. The boat quickly overturned, and the sailors were pounded and pulverized on the bar—then swept out to sea. On seeing their comrades in distress, the gallant crew of the *Astrolabe*'s long boat attempted a rescue and suffered the same fate. In minutes, twenty-one had perished. Neither wreckage nor bodies were recovered.

After making numerous scientific observations of local minerals, flora, fauna and Indigenous customs, the ships left those shores to explore our northern coast. La Pérouse was to spend only a few weeks off British Columbia. His log expresses continued frustration over the late summer fogs, which prevented detailed explorations much of the time. He was also concerned about missing the easterly trade winds from California to Asia.

"But a much more important consideration, the danger of missing the monsoon off China, induced me to abandon this research, to which we must have sacrificed at least six weeks, on account of the precautions necessary in this kind of navigation, which ought only to be undertaken in the longest and finest days of the year. A whole season would scarcely suffice for such a[n] expedition which ought to be the object of a separate voyage…"

Still, he made some important realizations on his way to Monterey. In mid-August he cruised by and named the Kerouard Islands—Haida Gwaii. La Pérouse seemed uncertain about the true nature of Vancouver Island. When he crossed its northern tip in heavy fog he referred to it as part of the "continent," but his chart and log shows an ambiguous dotted line between Vancouver Island and the mainland rather than a solid line usually used to indicate the coast. With a bit more time and clearer weather, this expedition would likely have discovered that Vancouver Island was not a peninsula but a separate island, predating Captain George Vancouver by six years. La Pérouse passed Nootka without landing due to fog on August 26 and was in Monterey Bay by September 14. The Spanish commander of the fort welcomed the explorers with great hospitality and helped them prepare for the next leg in their long journey.

From Monterey, the two ships headed west, never to return to the Americas. They arrived in Portuguese Macao in January but were unable to effect necessary repairs, so they sailed for Manila where resources of every kind were available. From Manila the two ships headed north, cruising close to Taiwan, the west coast of Japan and Siberia. The island of Sakhalin was extensively mapped and to everyone's surprise was found to be separate from the Japanese island of Hokkaido. By September 1787 they had reached Petropavlovsk Bay on Kamchatka and were warmly welcomed by the Russian governor, Barthelemy de Lesseps. One of the crew members who spoke Russian left the expedition and struck out overland with the expedition's journals, maps and observations. He arrived in Paris in 1789—the only member of the expedition to return to his native land.

With the weather swiftly deteriorating, La Pérouse turned south to the Samoan Islands. Again, tragedy struck. The handsome natives appeared friendly. Gifts were exchanged while water, pigs, coconuts, bananas and breadfruit were taken onboard. Yet great scars and wounds on the locals suggested a warlike nature. On December 11, Captain de Langle, the second in command, led two longboats and two pinnaces carrying sixty-one men into a charming, coral-filled cove to collect water. About two hundred Indigenous People gathered on the beach but the Frenchmen were armed and felt they had little to fear. After an hour the crowd had swelled to over fifteen hundred, crowding the beach and little creek. De Langle tried to defuse the situation by distributing gifts. Those who received a trinket were dissatisfied and those who received nothing were furious. The mariners retreated toward their boats, but a rapidly rising tide forced them to wade, which dampened their muskets and powder. When the French pushed off, the Samoans unleashed a deadly hail of stones fired by slings. Almost everyone was hit, and it became impossible to fight off the angry hoards while manoeuvring out of the narrow bay. Twelve were killed, including de Langle and the noted naturalist Lamanon. The remaining crew were forced to abandon the longboats, which momentarily diverted the attackers who ripped them apart. Racing the pinnaces, the men pitched the water barrels over the side and made a very narrow escape. When the two boats pulled alongside the frigates loaded with dead and wounded, a loud clamour rang out to turn the cannons on a group of innocent Samoans who'd been selling supplies from their canoes. La Pérouse would have none of it, but he did fire a cannon without shot, which quickly sent the canoes scurrying back to land. A retaliatory raid was planned for the bay where the attack took place but was cancelled when it was pointed out that if any of the boats ran aground on the treacherous coral reefs not a single man would survive.

Anxious to reach Botany Bay in Australia, La Pérouse spent little time charting other islands in Oceania. He stopped at the Niue and Tonga Islands, but after the recent disaster, caution kept him and his men from going ashore. On January 24, 1788, they arrived off Botany Bay and found to their surprise an English fleet anchored there. There were two warships, *Sirius* and *Supply* escorting penal transports with 1,017 prisoners and guards on board. By strange coincidence the expedition had arrived at exactly the same time as the British were establishing their first new colony in Australia for deported convicts. Happily, Commodore Phillip and his English officers offered every assistance and agreed to deliver the French admiral's reports to his homeland. A few days later, the La Pérouse expedition departed Botany Bay and disappeared.

In 1791 a search party composed of two French frigates was sent to find the lost explorers. They stopped at Tonga, New Caledonia and the New Hebrides but found nothing. They also passed a small island 1,400 miles northeast of Australia called Vanikoro, but heavy seas prevented a landing. All further searches were brought to a halt by the chaos and devastation of the French Revolution and the Napoleonic Wars. In the mid-1820s numerous artifacts of French origin began to appear on the trading markets around the New Hebrides. Among the items was a battered silver sword hilt with the initials of La Pérouse. The East Indian lascar (seaman) who'd traded the hilt claimed to have met two very old men in 1820 who'd been sailors on the lost ships. He added that much of the wreckage could still be seen on Vanikoro, and some was still salvageable.

So much interest was generated that the British East India Company sent a Captain Dillon to investigate in the ship *Research*. With offers of large quantities of glass beads, hardware and cloth, he was able to collect a variety of items from the Indigenous people and from the neighbouring reef. Among the items recovered were cast-iron cooking pots, hooks, bolts, ironwork, four bronze swivel guns, a large French naval bell, a millstone, pieces of scientific instruments and a fir plank decorated with a fleur-de-lis, which had been used as a door panel by the local people. Dillon returned the artifacts to France and the plank was positively identified as a fragment from the taffrail on one of the La Pérouse ships. The captain received a hero's welcome in Paris and was presented to King Charles X.

So what happened to the ill-fated expedition? Not surprisingly, the local inhabitants showed great reticence in discussing the incident and the two aged sailors never resurfaced. However, the scenario may have gone something like this. The *Boussole* and *Astrolabe* had just arrived and anchored off Vanikoro when a big storm blew up and drove both vessels aground. The local people massed on the beach and perhaps fired a few desultory arrows at the stricken ships. Remembering the disaster on Samoa, the crew of one of the vessels panicked and replied to the arrows with cannon fire. When the ship finally broke up on the reef the survivors were summarily executed as they reached the beach.

Fortunately, the other ship—probably the *Boussole*—commanded by La Pérouse, was resting on a sandy bottom and responded to the arrows with peace offerings of hatchets, beads and cloth. When the wind died down an old chief paddled out to the ship. He was treated kindly and given many gifts. Hostilities ended, the vessel was unloaded, and many valuable supplies were recovered. After several long and fruitless years waiting for rescue, the majority of survivors constructed a longboat from the wreckage, sailed off into the sunset and were never seen again. A few chose to remain on Vanikoro where they probably inter-married and acted as mercenaries for the local chieftains, surviving well into the 1820s, almost forty years after the expedition set out.

One can't help wondering about our selective ignorance concerning the La Pérouse expedition. Why is this fascinating and haunting tale of explorations so little known, while others are endlessly drummed into our heads? A couple of thoughts come to mind. The long period of revolution and warfare that engulfed Europe and much of the rest of the world occupied centre stage between 1789 and 1815. What could compare with the drama and carnage of the Battles of Austerlitz, Trafalgar, Borodino and Waterloo, among many others? By the time the mystery was solved years later, nobody but the French really cared.·

Then, too, consider that both Canada and the US are children of the British Empire, with the same language, literature and history. This English-speaking bias has sometimes left us sadly ignorant of other important world events. Incredible as it may seem, only one abridged translation of La Perouse's *A Voyage Round the World Performed in the Years 1785, 1786, 1787 and 1788* was published in North America before the 1960s. And that was in 1801.

WHO SHOT ESTEVAN LIGHT?

The conspiracy theory that the Allies attacked Estevan
Lighthouse is as silly as it sounds. For many westerners it
was just too hard to believe that the Japanese had the intelligence and technical ability to launch this attack. How
wrong they were. The Allies had no reason to stir up more
war fever. The Japanese were running rampant in Southeast Asia, China and Pearl Harbor. Hitler was tearing up
Europe and had just declared war on the United States.
The shelling of the lighthouse was a very minor sideshow
in the widening war.

As summer's dusk settled slowly over the lighthouse at Estevan Point
on that memorable night of June 20, 1942, keeper Robert Lally happened to stare out to sea. In the distance, off to the southwest, he made
out a "warship zigzagging under heavy smokescreen." The sight was not
uncommon during the early days of the war as Canadian naval crews
based at Esquimalt frequently trained in these waters. But when the shells
began to fly at the big light, Lally realized that this was no training mission.
Within minutes of the attack, the keeper had rushed up the 45-metre lighthouse tower and extinguished the powerful beacon. He then stepped out
onto the cupola and, from this ringside seat, observed the attack. The shells
arrived, at first 500 metres out, then 350, closer and closer. At least six
shells landed in front of the light, while others roared over the tower like
"freight trains passing over a bridge" and exploded near the First Nations
village of Hesquiat. In all, about seventeen large shells were fired, although
some observers later reported as many as twenty-five. Witnesses were un-
clear as to how many vessels took part in the shelling; many identified the
attacker as a large submarine, probably Japanese; some thought they saw
other ships as well. There were no injuries and damage was surprisingly
slight: only a few windows in the tower were broken by flying debris. The
terrified Indigenous population at Hesquiat fled by boat into the protection of Hesquiat harbour. Civilians at the lighthouse were evacuated into
the darkening bush in case of a land invasion, while the rest of the staff
stolidly remained at their posts.

Fears of a landing party or demolition squad proved groundless: the
intruders vanished as silently as they had arrived. Over the next few weeks,

The lighthouse was reputedly shelled by a Japanese submarine in 1942—or was it an inside job by the Allies to whip up war enthusiasm? Image credit: Living Cowichan via Wikimedia Commons, public domain

authorities examined the evidence, including craters, metal fragments and a dud shell. It was quickly concluded that the fire had come from the 14-cm gun of a Japanese submarine—the first enemy attack on Canadian soil since the War of 1812.

Defences at the isolated lighthouse were beefed up and life soon returned to normal. There the matter rested for more than forty years.

Then, in 1985, lightkeeper Donald Graham published *Keepers of the Light,* a book about British Columbia's lighthouses that soon became a classic. In his chapter on the Estevan Point lighthouse, he argued convincingly that the attack had nothing to do with a Japanese submarine. Some eyewitnesses had claimed that at least two large vessels were conducting the shelling, but Graham ridiculed the notion that the Estevan light was a credible military target for anyone. In fact, he argued that it would actually be an aid to enemy navigators. And how could the "gunners get twenty-five straight misses around that huge 150-foot tower, sticking out like a clay pipe in a shooting gallery?" No, it was not the Japanese. Rather, Graham suggested, it was a covert operation undertaken by the federal government (perhaps in collusion with the United States) to unite Canada firmly behind the war effort. Canadian or American warships fired those shells harmlessly to scare the bejesus out of Canadians, and in particular, to wake up those reluctant Quebecois and other "lukewarm patriots" to the very real dangers of the deepening war. Shadowy RCMP officers reportedly threatened dismissal or prison terms to any witnesses at Estevan who disputed the official version of the incident. The dud shell bore Japanese ideographs in yellow paint, but according to Graham, the lightkeeper also claimed that English "markings, numerals and whatever" were stamped on the base of the shell. And the entry for June 20, 1942, in Lally's official lightkeeper's logbook has mysteriously disappeared.

Even the American intelligence personnel who compiled the official record after the war, using confiscated Japanese documents, felt the sting of Graham's contempt. Commander Yokoda's description of submarine I-26's attack on Estevan was summarily dismissed as a sore loser's evil nonsense: "Yokoda was a questionable confessor at best. There's no more despicable trade in warfare than commanding a submarine. It takes a man with a shrivelled soul to peer through a periscope, put the profile of an unarmed merchant ship on the open sea behind the crosshairs, and order torpedoes away. He can be sure there won't be many survivors." To cap this argument, Graham pointed out that on June 19, the day before the attack, Parliament was debating a contentious amendment to the 1940 National Mobilization Act, which would have permitted conscription. The shelling of Estevan, he claims, was used with great effect by proponents of the amendment and was instrumental in allowing the bill to pass final reading in July.

This "Great Canadian Conspiracy Theory" soon took on a life of its own. In 1994, CBC-TV aired a segment on *The Fifth Estate* that featured Donald Graham. Linden MacIntyre, host of the show, also interviewed two witnesses to the shelling: Myna Peet, then eight years old, and Robert Lally, Jr., about the same age. Then MacIntyre observed: "The Americans even trotted out a submarine commander, Minoru Yokoda, who boasted that he directed the shelling of Estevan Point... For Donald Graham it boiled down to a test of credibility. The war stories of a defeated Japanese submarine commander, against the eyewitness account of a lightkeeper with nothing to gain from embellishing what he saw." It is not surprising that many Canadians believe the attack on Estevan was a grand manipulation, an event staged by *agents provocateurs*—courtesy of the Canadian government.

Does this hypothesis hold up under careful scrutiny? There is a considerable body of evidence, ignored by both Donald Graham and *The Fifth Estate*, that a Japanese submarine did indeed attack Estevan lighthouse that night. A number of daring raids on the West Coast of North America were carried out by Japanese submarines in 1942. The effects were minimal, but the attacks represented a serious effort by the Imperial Japanese Navy to cause disruption along the West Coast and to sow fear and confusion. Within weeks after the bombing of Pearl Harbor, according to Bert Webber's book *Retaliation: Japanese Attacks and Allied Countermeasures on the Pacific Coast in World War II*, no fewer than nine Japanese submarines had arrived off the West Coast to attack shipping vessels moving between the Juan de Fuca Strait and San Diego. Only a handful of cargo ships were sunk before the Allies greatly increased their anti-submarine vigilance. Intense air and ship patrols made life so difficult for the Japanese raiders that military officials in Tokyo decided to take a more drastic step: direct attacks on the coast. On the evening of February 23, 1942, the Imperial Navy submarine I-17 surfaced off of Santa Barbara, California. Commander Kozo Nishino took the vessel past the resort town and up the Santa Barbara Channel for about 30 km to Ellwood, coming abreast of the Barnsdale Oil Company oil fields at about 7:00 p.m. The sub was only 1.5 km from shore when it lobbed twenty-five 14-cm shells at the oil installations in the space of twenty minutes.

On board I-17, the nine-man gun crew under gunnery officer Lieutenant Shimada worked methodically loading, aiming and firing their heavy weapon, while anti-aircraft crews, expecting an air attack at any moment, hovered nervously over two 25-mm machine guns. When the shelling ended, the big sub headed west and slipped silently out to sea. According to Webber's *Retaliation*, US Navy radio operators intercepted a coded report sent to Emperor Hirohito later that night, which claimed that Santa Barbara was "a seething mass of flame, with wild panic visible on-shore." Miraculously, damage to the refinery was estimated at only $500. Two dozen oil workers escaped unhurt, and no fires were started. A pier, oil derrick and local land values were the only casualties. But fear is quick-ly contagious, and panic erupted across Los Angeles the next evening as jittery anti-aircraft crews cruised the skies searching for Japanese bombers. On the way home, I-17 sank two cargo ships within a week. The Allies had their revenge: eighteen months later, on August 19, 1943, I-17 met her end off New Caledonia during a running surface battle with a New Zealand minesweeper and two US Navy planes. Out of a crew of ninety-four, six were rescued.

Four months later, according to the *New York Times*, the Imperial Navy shrewdly planned a double hit to achieve maximum psychological effect: Estevan was to be shelled on June 20 by Captain Minoru Yokoda and the crew of I-26, and on the next night Fort Stevens, a US Army fort at the mouth of the Columbia River near Astoria, Oregon, was to be shelled by Meiji Tagami and the crew of I-25. The attack on Estevan was carried out on June 20 as scheduled. The following evening at 11:30 p.m., shells pasted the beach between Fort Stevens and the small vacation community of Seaside, Oregon, leaving seventeen 1.5-m craters. Captain Tagami of I-25 began firing from an extreme range of 13,000 metres, with a water depth of only 30 metres. Because he was using a very old American chart, he mistakenly thought that the fort housed a submarine base. Tagami was also unaware that Battery Russell had the only operational 10-inch guns at Fort Stevens. Fortunately for him they were not pressed into service that night: little damage was done to the base. Nearby residents of Astoria were shaken from their beds by the loud explosions, and hundreds of people watched a spectacular light show far out at sea each time the gun fired. But instead of panicking, most witnesses seemed to revel in the excitement. "The Japs picked a swell place for harmless target practice," one resident commented cheerfully to a reporter. Colonel Doney, spokesman for the US Army, unequivocally blamed a submarine for the attack. He noted that the shell fragments found in the craters had come from high-velocity, low-trajectory shells that appeared to have been fired from several kilome-tres offshore. The sub drifted or sailed about 5 km during the bombard-ment. Doney added that an air search for the invader was under way. That search was unsuccessful.

Just hours after the incident in Oregon and barely a day after the shelling at Estevan, Radio Tokyo trumpeted a great naval victory over Canada and America. According to Domei, the official radio news agency of wartime Japan, important military installations in both countries had been destroyed by submarine bombardment, causing dismay and confusion along the entire defence perimeter of the West Coast. Citizens from Alaska to Mexico were "panic stricken" by the attacks on Seaside and Estevan, and Canada in particular had been taught a painful lesson. Shelling the lighthouse was but "the first blow at the Canadian mainland... Thus Canada has been shown she is attacked by the Axis navies from the East as well as the West." The story pointed out that Estevan lay very close to Puget Sound and numerous important military bases; more raids should be expected. The attacks were so devastating, said the report, that the Allies would no longer be able to send supplies to Australia, and further air raids on the Japanese mainland were now completely out of the question. Japanese submarines in combination with the German U-boats in the Atlantic would also cut off supplies to the Russians, thereby preventing the opening of a second front in Europe. These claims were of course inflated by the hyperbole of wartime. But if the attack on Estevan came from Canada's own navy (with the possible help of the Americans), how would the propaganda spin masters at Domei, thousands of miles away, have found out the details so quickly, and used the information with such excellent timing?

The most audacious wartime attacks on North American soil were launched in September 1942. Japanese naval designers had long been fascinated by the idea of a submarine capable of carrying and launching an airplane. The I series, B class submarines used in all of the West Coast attacks were very large cruising boats, each with a watertight airplane hangar fore of the conning tower. They were 105 metres in length, they displaced 3,300 tonnes, and with a range of 25,000 km they could remain at sea for ninety days without servicing. As well, a small float plane provided eyes for the sub (there was no radar on Japan's submarines until much later). Code-named GLEN by the Allies, the little float plane was a marvel of compactness and ingenuity. The fuselage, wings, floats and fins were detachable and divided into twelve connecting pieces. Flaps and tail folded neatly to fit into the cramped cylindrical hangar of the conning tower. Powered by a small 340 hp radial engine, the stubby plane had a top speed of 150 knots and an endurance of about five hours. Its battle load consisted of a small machine gun and two 76-kg bombs—if intercepted, GLEN would have been no match for Allied fighters. Preparation for launching via the compressed air catapult took a tedious hour, as did recovery, which was carried out with a special crane located on the foredeck.

Following the attacks on Estevan and Seaside, the two submarines returned to Yokosuka submarine base in Japan for supplies. Then, according to Flight Warrant Officer Nobuo Fujita, I-25 sailed back to the West Coast in early September for what Japan hoped would be the most provocative attacks of all. At dawn on September 9, Fujita loaded two incendiary bombs onto his float plane and catapulted off the deck of I-25. Accompanied by petty officer Shoji Okuda, he flew his GLEN low over the well-lighted Oregon coast, dropping his bombs in the large forests 80 km inland near Brookings, Oregon. An alert forest ranger noticed the mysterious dawn raider, with an engine that sounded like a "model A Ford hitting on three cylinders." He quickly located and doused the flames. When the float plane returned to the waiting sub, it was taken aboard just in time. An American A-29 Hudson bomber with British markings had sighted I-25; it dove and strafed the vessel with 135-kg bombs. I-25 was severely shaken, but only slightly damaged.

Three weeks later Fujita repeated his air attack 18 km east of Port Orford, Oregon, at around midnight. There is no confirmation that the bombs even exploded, and no fires spread into the damp underbrush. Fujita, who had experienced the Doolittle bombing raid firsthand in April 1942, later recalled: "That pilot had bombed my homeland for its first time. Now I was bombing his. It gave me great satisfaction." On their return flight, the aviators were led astray by a malfunctioning compass.

> Suddenly I remembered our compass trouble after the Sidney [Australia] reconnaissance. I pulled the Zero [not to be confused with the famous Zero fighter] into a quick turn, and headed directly for the Cape Blanco lighthouse. It could mean interception, but I didn't care. At least I could then die gloriously, crashing into an enemy place. I might even dive into the lighthouse. Anything, to do the enemy damage through my death, and make it mean something, rather than just waiting for death to find me.

Instead, at the last minute, the two crew members decided to try once more to rendezvous 40 km offshore. Fortunately, I-25 was leaking a streak of oil, which led them to the sub and thus saved their lives.

For some months after the Port Orford incident, the Americans remained puzzled about the little float plane. Almost all civilians of Japanese descent had been interned in resettlement camps in the distant interior; there was concern that some had been missed. Could the GLEN have been launched from one of the countless lakes in the Pacific Northwest—final proof of a fifth column of Japanese traitors loose on the mainland?

Weeks of hard slogging through the bush produced no results. A search reported: "We found beautiful mountains, beautiful lakes, good fishing, tall wonderful trees, and mosquitoes and sore, wet feet. We didn't find any Japs." On July 11, 1943, I-25 was sunk in the Solomon Islands by the American destroyer USS *Taylor*.

Since the first wave of doubt immediately after the Santa Barbara/ Fort Stevens shellings and Fujita's bombings, no one has suggested that they were anything other than the work of Japanese submarines. The evidence on both sides of the Pacific is irrefutable. It should not be so difficult to believe that the very similar attack on Estevan was also made by the Imperial Navy, especially when veteran Japanese submariners themselves confirm it. In researching *Retaliation*, author Bert Webber made every effort to contact surviving Japanese submariners in the early 1970s and to get them to talk about the war. Most of them had been killed in battle, and some of those who survived were reluctant to talk about their experiences because western writers had misquoted them and treated them with contempt. But Webber did interview several retired Japanese submariners, including Commander Minoru Yokoda of I-26, who remained silent until 1973. But his memory of the Estevan shelling was still clear.

> It was evening when I shelled the area with about 17 shots. Because of the dark, our gun crew had difficulty in making the shots effective. At first the shells were way too short, not reaching shore. I remember vividly my yelling at them. Raise the gun! Raise the gun! To shoot at a higher angle. Then the shells went too far over the little community toward the hilly area. Even out at sea we could hear the pigs squealing as the shells exploded. [Yokoda may have heard harbour seals, which bark, bray, hoot and bellow when disturbed.] As I watched from the I-26, the people were very quick to put out the lights in the buildings but the lighthouse was slow to respond—the last light to turn off.

There is no boasting in this fascinating account, as Donald Graham suggests. On the contrary, the mission was a great disappointment to the Japanese commander, as he freely admitted. "There was not a single effective hit that night," he said. Similar stories were told by Nubuo Fujita and Commander Meiji Tagami of I-25, among others, and details of their stories have been corroborated by surviving crew members.

The Great Canadian Conspiracy theorists have glossed over or ignored other inconsistencies. First, the Estevan lighthouse was no small mom-and-pop operation in 1942. On the night of the shelling, there were twenty-two people at the isolated outpost—seventeen of them staff. The *New York Times* described Estevan as "one of the largest radio centers on the coast." It housed a telegraph, weather centre, lighthouse and powerful radio station to coordinate shipping throughout the north Pacific. The *Victoria Daily Times* observed:

> The irony of the shelling of Estevan lies in the fact that for the past 30 peacetime years the Estevan radio station has been giving complete radio services broadcasting weather conditions and handling air traffic generally for Japanese steamships which before the war were regularly operating in the trans-Pacific route. In fact, Estevan was an excellent military target, and the real question is why Canadian authorities had failed to realize this earlier and provide it with more protection.

Second, if the shelling of Estevan had been an elaborate setup designed to garner support for the war, local governments would have been informed of the ploy and would have made a big fuss over it. But just the opposite was true. After two days of headlines, the matter almost disappeared from view in both Canada and the USA. The mayor of Victoria remarked a day after the attack, "I haven't noticed any change in the people's demeanor… no one is jittery. Why should they be over a nuisance raid such as Estevan or Seaside?" When BC Premier John Hart was asked by reporters if he would issue a message calling for calm, he tartly responded, "No one has the jitters and it would be ridiculous to suggest they needed such a message." Even the *Toronto Globe and Mail* played it down. "This first attack on Canadian soil failed to cause any great excitement on the West Coast[,] made war conscious recently by the sinking of a United States merchant ship off Neah Bay just fifty-nine miles west of Victoria and by the landing of Japanese forces in the outer fringe of the Aleutian Islands far to the northwest." The page two headline declared: "Japs' Shelling Held Harmless." Even Prime Minister Mackenzie King seemed more concerned about the fall of the north African fortress of Tobruk than about Estevan. On June 23 he commented: "[I]t is as critical a situation in the Middle East as has arisen since the war commenced. And there have been other evidences in the past forty-eight hours that in this world-encircling conflict Canada is coming more and more into the zone of immediate danger."

Third, the war was going disastrously for the Allies in the early summer of 1942. Tobruk fell to General Irwin Rommel on the same day as the Estevan incident. Twenty-five thousand British soldiers were taken prisoner along with the mountains of supplies, enough to keep Afrika Korps plentifully supplied for almost a year. In Russia, the German steamroller was driving deep into the south. The huge fortress of Sebastopol in the Crimea fell on July 3, after a siege of 250 days, with a loss of a hundred thousand Russian soldiers and thousands of tanks and guns. The Don River was breached the next day, and on July 7, Voronezh surrendered. In the Atlantic, German U-boats were sinking vital convoy ships many times faster than they could be built. In 1942 alone, more than fifteen hundred ships with gross tonnage of 6,226,215 were lost to submarines—while U-boat operational strength in the Atlantic surged from 91 to 212. Winston Churchill later wrote, "The U-boat attack of 1942 was our worst evil." In the Pacific, the Japanese occupied Attu, Kiska and Aggatu in the Aleutians by early June, and seemed poised to strike both Alaska and northern British Columbia. With all of this very genuine bad news, there was really no need for any Canadian or American government to stage a phony attack on Estevan.

An interesting question does remain. How does one explain the sightings of several vessels acting in concert off Estevan that night? For days after the shellings, the Allies combed the seas for a "surface raider" or two submarines, which were never found. The observers' stories varied on the West Coast, visibility at dusk in misty June is notoriously poor, and Robert Lally, a key witness, had no binoculars. Contrary to what was reported by both Donald Graham and *The Fifth Estate*, most of the eyewitnesses reported only a single submarine in the deepening dusk. According to Edward T. Redford, the experienced Officer in Charge, who had lost an arm in World War I:

> The submarine surfaced about two miles offshore and was plainly visible. Shelling commenced at approximately 9:40 pm and continued for about 40 minutes. The first shells landed on the beach about 100 yards in front of the lighthouse. Mr. Lally, who was the lightkeeper at the time, immediately put out the light. The sub apparently then raised its sights, for from then on the shells went overhead... The submarine pulled out on the surface and everyone could see her and hear the diesel engines quite clearly. While naturally there was some nervousness, everyone, including women and children, took the whole incident in their stride, then spent the following day souvenir hunting.

Captain James L. Detwiler of HMCS *San Tomas* later interviewed an Indigenous woman from Hesquiat. "She was sincere," he reported, "and tried to make me understand that she knew the difference between a whale and a boat. She said that she first thought it was a whale, but when it didn't splash or 'blow' she knew it was a boat."

Mrs. Lally, wife of the lightkeeper, had this to say:

> Canadian warships passed the lighthouse almost daily. I saw two early in the morning of the shelling, so the sound of gun-fire that night didn't bother me. I thought it was target prac-tice. I was just putting the youngest of the children to bed when the first shell exploded on the beach. "That's pretty poor shooting! It came pretty close," I yelled to my husband who had just come down from turning on the lighthouse for the night. "Get the hell out of here! It's a Jap sub and they are shelling the lighthouse!" my husband Mike shouted back. More shells sailed overhead.

All of the eyewitness accounts that night must be taken with a grain of salt. Visibility was just too poor, and the imagination can play strange tricks in times of stress, particularly when events are recalled years later. The spectacular light show produced by the submarine's 14-cm gun, as well as her large and noisy presence, may well have impaired the witnesses' ability to observe events coolly and objectively. Certainly there was a wide variety of conflicting accounts of that exciting evening.

The five submarine attacks on North America demonstrated the weaknesses as well as the strengths of the Imperial Navy's submarine ser-vice. Navigating those thousands of kilometres, endless searches of track-less Pacific expanse for months at a time, launching and recovering float planes at night, and evading endless searches demanded courage, disci-pline and competence. Yet nothing of importance was accomplished. The attacks were too sporadic and too far apart to make much of an impression, and the marksmanship was abysmal. No doubt the Japanese were hope-ful of creating the same kind of sensation that Doolittle's B-25 bombing raid had generated in Japan. But as the war deteriorated for the Japanese, their subs were called back to protect her navy in the home islands; by September 1942, they had left our Pacific coasts forever. Many ended up as supply vessels serving isolated island garrisons in the Pacific. The clear and shallow waters surrounding these islands provided little protection for large submarines. Most were soon lost, and the morale of the Imperial submarine service plummeted.

The Japanese never learned to use their submarines as effectively as other countries during the war. The military also grossly underestimated the danger of Allied submarine fleets and paid a heavy price because of that error in judgement. Half of Japan's maritime tonnage lost was to submarines. American and German submariners sank anything that could carry a cargo, but the Japanese never developed the submarine "wolf pack" hunting technique essential for systematic destruction of the Allies' commerce fleet. After 1942, the huge volume of cargo vessels running between the mainland and the Pacific war zone was left almost untouched. Instead, the Imperial Navy concentrated its strategic thinking on capital warships.

Japanese submarine commanders were given a strict priority list of what to attack, carriers first, battleships second, cruisers third, and so on. Merchant ships could only be targeted if there were no other warships in the area. There were even stipulations on how many torpedoes could be expended on each type of target. Fire everything if you faced a battleship, three at a cruiser and only one at a cargo vessel.

Bushido, the Samurai code of honour, may well have been a factor in these policies. Bushido taught that it was morally wrong to attack non-combatants randomly. War was fought between warriors who were expected never to surrender and to die for their cause if necessary. Blowing a helpless cargo carrier to kingdom come simply did not fit in with this code of ethics. Interestingly, Bushido may have also played a role in the selection of west coast targets in 1942. After the war ended, Captain Ryonosuka Imamura, Secretary to the Japanese Naval Ministry, was asked why more populated targets had not been chosen. He replied, "You ask why we didn't shell some coastal United States city rather than Fort Stevens and [the] Santa Barbara oil tanks. At Santa Barbara it was our decision to shell oil tanks because we felt them important war assets. So it was with Fort Stevens. We didn't use these attacks to terrorize your people, but to strike war blows."

There can be little doubt that a Japanese submarine attacked the Estevan complex in June 1942. In his appearance on *The Fifth Estate*, Donald Graham argued convincingly that in wartime, governments manipulate and even create news for propaganda purposes. Two good examples are the phony Gulf of Tonkin incident in 1964, and stories of Iraqi soldiers removing Kuwaiti babies from maternity wards in 1990. But the theory that the Estevan shelling was nothing more than a setup cannot be supported by the evidence: physical traces, eyewitness accounts, submariners' stories and information on other Japanese military activities in the Pacific all contradict the theory.

And so does Canadian history. Graham's contention that the attack played a major role in the conscription debate is a weak one. The ambiguous results of the conscription plebiscite held on April 27, 1942, led Prime

Minister Mackenzie King to waffle and delay any action for as long as possible. "Not necessarily conscription but conscription if necessary " neatly defined (or obscured) the issue. Every Canadian male over age sixteen had to register for national service, but only volunteers were sent to the front. Not until 1944, when the Allies suffered heavy losses in Italy and France did King send the "Zombies" (the new recruits) to fight overseas.

No one can know every detail of what happened at Estevan Point on June 20, 1942. But the evidence shows that there was no political conspiracy: a Japanese submarine attacked Estevan, as well as four other sites on the West Coast of North America during the spring and summer of 1942.

Sources:

Fukita, Nobua and Joseph D. Harrington, "I bombed the USA," in US Naval Institute Proceedings, June 1961, pp. 64–69.

Graham, Donald, *Keepers of the Light*. Madeira Park, BC: Harbour Publishing, 1985.

New York Times, June 22, 1942, p. 9.
Toronto Globe and Mail, June 22, 1942, p. 1.
Victoria Daily Colonist, June 22, 1942, p. 5.
Victoria Daily Times, June 22, 1942, p. 1.

Webber, Bert. *Retaliation: Japanese Attacks and Allied Countermeasures on the Pacific Coast in World War II*. Corvallis: Oregon State University Press, 1975.

Webber, Bert. *Silent Siege III. Japanese Attacks on North America in World War II*. Medford, Oregon: Webb Research Group, 1997.

AFLAME IN THE WATER:
THE FINAL CRUISE OF THE *GRAPPLER*

The sinking of the *Grappler* was a monumental disaster in
which everything that could go wrong did so with a ven-
geance. The fire, darkness, language difficulties, the greed
of the captain and crew, and the age of the *Grappler* itself
all contributed to the disaster. It's a miracle that anyone
survived. The information for this story came from newspapers of the day and the coroner's report.

On the night of April 29, 1883, the steamer *Grappler* burned and sank
in Seymour Narrows with a loss of over a hundred passengers. It was
the worst fire aboard ship in British Columbia's maritime history, yet it remains little known. The tragedy entailed a shameful combination of poor
planning, panic and cowardice, but from it arose the beginnings of safety
regulations on the West Coast.

The *Grappler* was originally built in 1857 as a Royal Navy gunboat
designed to patrol the shallow rivers of the Black Sea during the Crimean
War—which was over by the time it was launched. HMS *Grappler* was a
handy little steamship—32 metres long, 6 metres wide, with a draught of
only 2 metres. On the cutting edge of the technology of the day, it was
powered by a 60 nominal hp reciprocating engine (about 240 of today's
horsepower), driving a screw propeller, which pushed it along at a steady
6.5 knots. When the winds were fair, a fore and aft square rig turned the
vessel into an adequate sailer. *Grappler* was also well armed, with two of the
Royal Navy's most modern breech-loading guns on revolving carriages. Its
very name suggested determination and aggression, and several examples
of the type were built with similar names including HMS *Forward*.

With the end of the conflict in the Crimea, Britain looked for a place
where the mobility and power of these gunboats could be put to good use.
Accordingly, in 1859, *Grappler* and *Forward* were both dispatched to the
uncharted coastal waters of British Columbia to counter "Indian threats"
and growing American influence in the area. Both gunboats were busy
over the next nine years, enforcing law and order, rigorously suppressing
any sign of Indigenous rebellion and holding the line against American
ambitions in the Northwest.

The HMS *Grappler* was Britain's muscle on the West Coast during the mid-19th century, suppressing "Native" threats, quelling a miners' strike, and opposing American influence. Painting by Bill Maximick, "Grappler Arrives at Komoux"

Their most noteworthy moment came during the Lamalcha incident in April 1863. The *Forward* was attempting to apprehend the murderers of three white settlers when it was repulsed with a hail of bullets from the fortified First Nations village of Lamalcha on Kuper Island. A "boy second class" seaman was killed, and the Royal Navy suffered a major loss of face. Two weeks later both *Grappler* and *Forward* returned to the village and, finding it deserted, burned it to the ground along with several canoes. A large naval force, including the two gunboats, was then quickly assembled to track down the murder suspects hiding on the neighbouring islands. The *Grappler* also served the fledgling coal industry by delivering militia to suppress a bitter, four-month strike against Dunsmuir, Diggle and Company in Nanaimo.

These small warships, crowded and uncomfortable, were not popular with their crews. With the machinery and boilers taking up over half the space between decks, the crew of thirty-six squeezed into what remained at the extremities, officers aft, the men forward. Even in an age when seamen had nothing in the way of luxuries afloat, life on these little craft was well below the already low standard.

By 1868, the boilers of both ships were deemed too worn out for repair and they were auctioned off. The *Forward* was sold for $7,000 to agents acting for a Mexican firm. During a period of revolution in that country in the 1870s, it was captured by rebels and burned. The *Grappler*, being in worse shape, fetched only $2,400. The new owners thought the ship would be perfect for the rapidly expanding coastal trade. For the next seven years the *Grappler* led a varied career as a freighter jack-of-all-trades, passing through several owners. In late 1875, the steamer was purchased by the famous American captain, William Moore, later to be one of the first sourdoughs of the Klondike. Moore proved a better gold digger than shipping tycoon, as the vessel soon became involved in a number of dangerous and unlucky incidents—a portent of the future.

In March of 1876 the *Grappler* went aground on Beacon Rock in Nanaimo Harbour and was beached on the mud flats of the Millstone River for repairs. It was soon aground again, on Sidney Spit near Victoria, causing one shipbuilder to dismiss the vessel as "rotten." However, a steamship inspector disagreed, pronouncing it "sound, staunch, and seaworthy in every respect." Then in July, while towing the barque *Henry Bruce*, it ran up on D'Arcy Island. The heavy towing rope pulled the *Grappler* over onto its starboard beam, filling it with water, and the old gunboat remained on the rocks for another three weeks.

In November 1880, the ship was hauling a load of heavy machinery from Victoria to Nanaimo when it encountered a fierce southeast gale. The battered hull sprang a leak and the *Grappler* barely made it to Northwest Bay before sinking to its guardrails. Miraculously, the crew was able to patch the hole, and the tug *Pilot* pulled it to safety during a lull in the storm. These repeated groundings undoubtedly played a role in the final tragedy. Although the hull and boiler remained certified, the boiler and firebox had been set in brickwork that may have been fatally weakened by this series of mishaps. In late April 1883, the *Grappler* departed Victoria for points north with a crew of about eight whites and several Indigenous coal carriers. The captain, John F. Jagers, was experienced, having served as mate and then master of the Hudson's Bay Company *Beaver*. The old gunboat was packed to bursting with lumber, cannery supplies, 50 kegs of blasting powder, thirty white passengers, and more than a hundred Chinese cannery workers. On April 29, the *Grappler* docked in Departure Bay to take on 40 tons of coal and unload the blasting powder—a good thing, as it turned out. Anxious to maintain schedule, the ship took on a new pilot and was back on its way by 4:00 p.m.

At about 10:00 p.m. during slack tide with a calm sea, the steamer was plodding toward Seymour Narrows and approaching the infamous Ripple Rock, when the mate reported "the smell of fire." Most of the white passengers were sleeping in the few staterooms and temporary berths between decks, while the Chinese had stretched out on the freight wherever they could. Captain Jagers went forward and opened the hatch for inspection. "I went below and found a strong smell of fire, but no flame; I went from the after part of the ship along the boiler to the forward part of the ship to the back connection of the boiler. I smelt smoke: I naturally went to look for fire where there was most heat... I went to call the mate, and did not go below after that; I could not get down." Unfortunately, the brick firebox was inaccessible due to the heavy bulkheads and freight stored below. A large iron plate used for cooking was fitted over the firebox, and it was later surmised that something carelessly stowed had fallen on the plate. But spontaneous combustion in the coal bunkers or a coal oil lamp may also have been responsible.

Whatever the cause, the fire moved with horrifying speed. Crew members tried ineffectually to haul coal away from the spreading inferno but were quickly driven topside by the heat and smoke. Jagers ordered the hatches sealed, sounded five short blasts of the whistle, and set course for nearby Duncan Bay on Vancouver Island. "For God's sake, say nothing about it to the passengers—keep it quiet!" his first mate, John Smith, urged the captain. It was a strange and futile admonition, as the smoke, yelling, and clatter of running feet made it clear to all that something was going very wrong.

Attempts to fight the growing conflagration were seriously hindered by the darkness and lack of available equipment. Only a small lantern in the stern lit the scene; and buckets, hoses and axes were either missing or impossible to locate. James Jones, a passenger, reported:

> The crew were not sufficient; two hands, a mate, and an Indian were all that I saw. There was only one light in the after part of the boat; I did not hear anyone ask for lights until the time of the fire... There was no effort to stop the fire; there was hose, but I saw no water raised. I should judge there were 120 persons between decks; there was a hatchway aft, where it would be easy to escape; I can't say whether any went that way; by the other ways the passengers went over each other's heads. After the fire was discovered, it was about eight minutes until the ship was in flames.

It quickly became apparent that there was a severe shortage of lifejackets and lifeboat space aboard. *Grappler* had originally been equipped with three lifeboats, but the largest had been left in Victoria. Three flat-bottomed fishing skiffs stowed on deck were considered a sufficient replacement. Unfortunately, these ungainly boats were missing oars and oarlocks, and their draining plugs had been removed for the trip north. The remaining two lifeboats had places for only twenty-two. Sixty life preservers were supposedly on board, but few of the survivors reported finding any.

Meanwhile the old gunboat was steaming on full ahead, completely out of control. The wheel ropes had burned through and the throttle controls were firmly jammed. Chaos reigned as everyone rushed the boats in a panic. Passenger Robert K. Hall described the scene.

> Men, some of them half-dressed running frantically to and fro, half bereft of reason, calling on others to save them, the cries of the horrified Chinamen adding to the fearful confusion…
>
> As fast as a boat was lowered, men jumped into it— whites, Chinese, Indians—the coolies actually attempting to save their property, throwing clothing and bags of rice into the boats which capsized almost as soon as they were lowered. I could see there was no chance of saving my life by these means and took a set of steps, made it fast to a line, and threw it overboard, allowing it to tow alongside. When I saw the vessel had become completely unmanageable and there was no possibility of running her ashore I dropped overboard, cast off the line and supported by the steps was rapidly borne away with the current.

The crew made little effort to organize an evacuation. David Jones and several panicked passengers attempted to launch boats from the speeding ship with predictable results.

> We swung the boat out, and started to lower her. They let go very quick at the forward tackle, and we could not clear the rope. The after fall fouled, and the boat hung at an angle, she was… 8 or 10 [feet above the water]. I said to somebody 'cut that fall.' After they cut it, the boat turned somersault; I came up and grasped a rope from the ship, and asked to be hauled up; they hauled me a short distance, and let me fall into the water again. I then struck out to swim to shore.

Henry McCluskey was awakened by his nephew and immediately ran on deck searching for a bucket and hoses. He found no hose and only one bucket, which was half full of fish soaking for the cook. McCluskey lashed two barrels together and was about to go over the side when "I saw Mr. Steel [the engineer] with one lifebuoy and one life-preserver. I said, 'you are pretty well fixed for life-preservers.' I did not ask for one; he said nothing. I saw one life-preserver on the captain; this was after I saw Mr. Steel with two life-preservers; I saw a deck-hand named Conlan with a life-preserver; that makes four, all the life-preservers I saw." Indeed Captain Jagers seemed more concerned with salvaging the ship's strongbox than with passengers. "I then told the captain it was getting warm and was time to be getting ashore. I saw the safe, at the end of the windlass, close to the captain. I saw something like a stocking with money in the captain's hand. When I said it was time to go, the captain said, 'I won't go yet'."

McCluskey then went looking for an axe to chop down the foremast, which would have floated fifteen to twenty persons, but he was forced to retreat before the flames and entered the water with no flotation. He swam partway to shore and came upon several men clinging to a spar. "Mr. Steel, with his life-preserver on, came up and got on the spar; then a Chinamen came and got on the spar; that made four altogether. I told the men who had life-preservers to get off and let the spar float lighter; they did not get off."

Fortunately, they were soon rescued by Captain John McAlister, one of the few heroes of this debacle. This experienced sea captain was on his way north to the fishing grounds as a passenger, and it was he who owned the three skiffs stowed on deck. He accompanied Captain Jagers below, and sizing up the situation, ran back on deck to organize a bucket brigade. When this proved impossible, McAlister raced forward and tipped one of his skiffs into the rushing sea. He jumped in after it, clambered aboard, and was soon followed by a white man and a Chinese man. They salvaged a bamboo cane and broom from floating debris and painfully began to paddle their way toward Quadra Island (then called Valdes Island), picking up "five or six men and two or three Chinamen," as the *Victoria Daily Colonist* later related. "Suddenly, without warning, The *Grappler* turned and bore directly down on their fragile craft, passing within a few yards and singeing all with her fiery breath. The steamer kept going backwards and forwards in an erratic manner, the passengers shrieking and yelling for assistance and the flames spreading rapidly over the vessel." The courageous McAlister ferried his passengers to shore, and immediately set out once again using broken bits of lumber for oars. He pulled aboard "a Chinamen, a Siwash, Steel, the engineer, and several other white men" and returned to shore to build a fire for the survivors. Further rescue attempts soon became impossible as the already desperate situation took a severe turn for the worse. At about 11:00 p.m. the tide began to ebb.

Even today, the tidal rips in Seymour Narrows run at over 15 knots, making it one of the most dangerous stretches of water on the coast. In

1883, Ripple Rock lay in the centre of the channel, creating a boiling maelstrom for the unwary or unlucky. (Ripple Rock was destroyed in 1958 with 1,237 tonnes of explosives.) As the tidal flow strengthened, the struggling survivors were relentlessly sucked into a frigid hell of roaring white rapids that had consumed many a full-sized ship over the years. David Brown clung to one of McAlister's upturned skiffs and drifted "among some Chinamen who were supporting themselves with various articles. Two or three grabbed my legs and I felt my hold slackening. I exerted all my strength and managed to free myself." However, on sighting an exhausted white man clinging to a plank, Brown helpfully pulled him aboard.

> I had long before this lost sight of the ill-fated *Grappler*, but my companion and I kept our spirits till we heard the roar of the rapids and felt the increased strength of the current. We were spun round and round in the whirlpools, sometimes under water and sometimes above, but held on like grim death. At last, about an hour after sunrise we drifted ashore on an island and were found in the afternoon by a couple of Indians in a canoe, who took us to a camp of loggers.
>
> Passenger John Cardano broke his arm trying to launch one of the boats. He described using his remaining fist to punch his way on board one of McAlister's skiffs, occupied by two terrified Chinese. Around midnight the steamer's engine finally stopped and the ship grounded near Duncan Bay "wrapped in flames from stem to stern." A number of small explosions were heard as the *Grappler* burned through most of the night.

This terrible disaster had many contributing factors—an irresponsible crew, the darkness of a cold April night, the dearth of lifejackets, buckets, axes, hoses and lifeboat space, the ship barrelling along out of control, the vicious tidal rapids—all combined at the worst possible place and time. The clash of language and culture between the scores of Chinese workers and the thirty-odd white passengers and crew then turned a very bad situation into a catastrophe. Most of the Chinese workers were very recent arrivals with little understanding of the language and customs of the new country. The resulting lack of communication between the two groups made it impossible to stem panic and issue coherent directions for firefighting and a safe evacuation.

British Columbia was wracked by racial tension in the early 1880s. Burgeoning mines, roads and railways required more manpower than the province could furnish, so contractors were forced to import large numbers of workers from China and other Asian countries. It was said that two Chinese miners could do the work of three white workers —and do it for less money per worker. The influx reached a peak in 1882 when 8,083 of these Chinese workers arrived in the province, compared to 6,679 white immigrants. An ugly racist backlash developed as white workers moved to secure their position in the workplace. The railway work camps in particular seethed with discontent, and less than two weeks after the disaster one Chinese man was killed and several critically injured in a violent confrontation at Camp 37 near Lytton. On the doomed *Grappler*, each race viewed the other as if from another planet, jabbering nonsense, worshipping false gods and looking to steal each other's livelihoods. With all these barriers, co-operation between the two groups was clearly impossible.

At dawn the next day, McAlister made his way to the Kwakwa̲ka'wakw village near Cape Mudge for help. Canoes were immediately sent out to scour the beaches, and the survivors were brought back to the village, where they were very well treated before being transferred by steamer to Nanaimo. Twenty-one white men, two First Nations men and only thirteen Chinese men survived the sinking. Ten to twelve whites and about a hundred Asian passengers perished, but the true number is unknown because there was no official passenger list and many bodies were never recovered. One crew member was lost. At the inquest, even Captain Jagers seemed to have had little idea as to how many were on board at the time. "I think I had 100 passengers as near as I can tell, besides those belonging to the ship; I suppose there were about 30 white men and 70 Chinamen…" As we have seen, a passenger estimated 120 were between the decks before the fire. More would have been topside.

The hulk of the *Grappler* was found drifting with the tide, its hull burned to the waterline, and "thin as a wafer." It remained afloat for another half hour while Indigenous people from Salmon River clambered aboard to salvage what they could. Of particular concern was the ship's safe, which was said to contain at least $1,000. The First Nations people found and hauled out the strongbox, and $170.50 was salvaged in "half-melted silver coinage." The remainder, no doubt safe in Captain Jagers' sock, was never recovered. *Grappler* then suddenly flooded and sank, almost taking two Indigenous people along with it. It went down in 30 fathoms, about 1.5 km southeast of Ripple Rock. The next day the receiver of wrecks arrived and thanked the First Nations people for their kindness and gallant service.

Almost immediately, questions were raised about the safety of the vessel and the competence of its crew. Although most of the victims were

Chinese, it was the death of passenger Donald McPhail that prompted a coroner's inquest. After several days of testimony from survivors (no Chinese or Indigenous people were called), the jurors concluded that McPhail had died by drowning caused by the "accidental burning" of the ship. Arthur Vipond, BC's inspector of steamships, noted that the *Grappler* and her boiler had been examined just a few months before and found sound. "I should think the *Grappler*, as to her hull and machinery, at the time I inspected her, was fit to carry passengers, but not as to her equipment." Captain Jagers lost credibility when he revealed that his mate certificate had been confiscated. "I have lost it; not in this country." Under no legal obligation, he declined to tell the jurors when, where or how. Jagers noted that there were few requirements for operating a passenger vessel in British Columbia waters, and that, as captain, he needed neither a mate's licence nor a certificate from the Board of Trade. In fact, ship passenger travel was almost completely unregulated in the province.

The coroner's report, while critical of the captain and crew, was not damning in its findings. No serious laws had been broken, and the steamship line was neither fined nor required to pay compensation. The coroner ruled that the ship was not licensed to carry passengers, and that it had not made sufficient provision for their safety. The owners and officers were found to be "guilty of culpable negligence in allowing said steamer to leave this port in the condition she was, and [we] respectfully call the attention of the Government to the absolute necessity of having a duly authorized Inspector appointed for that purpose." That was the one positive outcome of this tragedy: the lackadaisical approach to safety at sea, and the absence of regulations and inspections for passenger vessels was no longer acceptable. Marine transportation was rapidly growing in British Columbia and had become too important to be left to chance. No more catastrophes on this scale would be tolerated.

Captains in Conflict

Public accusations of drunkenness and incompetence between rival west coast mariners raised eyebrows around the world, drawing attention to the riches of the BC coast.

The unexpected return of Captain James Cook's third expedition to the Scottish harbour at Stromness in the summer of 1780 created a sensation. The *Resolution* and *Discovery* had been absent for four years and three months, the longest single voyage of exploration ever. Most had given up on the explorers long before. Sadly, the great navigator himself did not survive the voyage, being attacked and dismembered at Kealakekua Bay (Hawai'i) during an altercation over the theft of the *Discovery*'s longboat. The main goal of the long voyage, discovery of the fabled Northwest Passage, had been unachievable. But Cook and his crew had navigated and mapped a vast part of the Pacific, from Northern California to the Bering Strait, a stunning accomplishment.

The voyage to these faraway lands generated tremendous interest and curiosity seekers besieged the crew looking for dried plants, bird skins, Indigenous artifacts, or any other souvenirs from the voyage. Of particular interest was the astronomical value in China of the beautiful pelts of an obscure west coast mammal called the sea otter. These strange creatures favoured the rocky shores of the open ocean from Baja to Alaska, and were "as plentiful as blackberries" off Vancouver Island. Cook's crew purchased about seventeen hundred of the best skins in Nootka as bedclothes, for a few pieces of scrap metal each. On arrival at Macao, the seamen were amazed to find these same skins worth upwards of fifty to seventy Spanish silver dollars—one went for $300. Two crew members from the *Resolution* were so addled by their good fortune that they made off with the ship's longboat intending to sail back to Nootka for another load. Neither was ever heard from again.

By any standard, China was the most civilized country on earth in the late 18th century. With a teeming population of over thirty million, the Manchu Dynasty was sophisticated, urbane, wealthy and almost entirely self-sufficient. Officially, the Celestial Empire neither needed nor wanted European goods, and trade with the *fanqwae*, or foreign devils, was strictly controlled. But one of the few items in great demand was the lustrous pelt from the sea otter, which was tailored into plush jackets for the wealthy and

Chief Maquinna gave his royal robe of sea otter skins to Captain James Cook, touching off a boom in the pelts with disastrous consequences for the BC marine ecosystem. Image credit: Maquinna, chief of the Nuu-chah-nulth people of Nootka Sound, Malaspina Expedition, 1789–94, drawing by Tomás de Suría (1761-1844), Museo de America-Coleccion, Madrid, Spain via Alamy

powerful. Sea otters were slow to reproduce and easy to hunt, so the supply of this "soft gold" never equalled demand, which led to ever escalating prices.

Several British raiding companies hurriedly organized to take advantage of the fabulous new China connections, but soon found themselves beset with bureaucratic obstacles. Chinese ports were closed to all outsiders except for Portuguese Macao. Even there, the old East India Company was the only British firm recognized by the Chinese, so all English ships at Macao had to first post bond with the company in order to access Chinese markets. On the supply end of the sea otter trade, the South Sea Company (famous for the South Sea Bubble, the first great stock market crash which bankrupted most of England in 1720) had secured monopoly rights for all British ships trading in the Pacific. This meant that English fur buyers in those waters had to first pay for an expensive licence from the company or be considered a poacher. Thus legitimate traders had to pay off two rapacious companies before they could sell a single skin in China. The only alternative was to enter a grey area in the law, and sail semi-legally as an adventurer under a Portuguese or Austrian flag of convenience. Such unwieldy restrictions hindered trade, and soon created a spirit of lawlessness that worked against both companies.

Among the first to obtain the two necessary licences was the London merchant firm of Richard Cadmon Etches. In 1785, the syndicate selected Nathaniel Portlock and George Dixon to take the 320-ton *King George* and 200-ton *Queen Charlotte* on a trading expedition to Nootka Sound and beyond. Both were experienced mariners who had accompanied Cook on his last voyage. The two were directed to revisit Nootka, explore new areas for trade, and see about constructing the first permanent European trading "factory" on the coast. They were not alone. The end of the American Revolution had led to the layoff of hundreds of highly qualified British and American officers and seamen now desperate to find employment in the merchant fleet. Most were more concerned about putting food on the table than the arcane niceties of the law. One of these scallywags was John Meares, a former Lieutenant in the Royal Navy, who found himself jobless in Calcutta. He was a handsome man without wealth, connections or experience, but was blessed with a brilliant talent for self-promotion. Meares had no trouble talking himself into a partnership and command of the *Nootka*, a 120-ton snow, which sailed for Alaska

John Meares was a former Royal Navy lieutenant without wealth, connections or experience. With a brilliant talent for self-promotion he talked himself into a partnership and the command of the *Nootka*. Image credit: W. Beechey, from *Voyages Made in the Years 1788 and 1789, from China to the North West Coast of America* via Wikimedia Commons, public domain

in February 1786 without papers. ["A snow had two masts, square rigged on both, with the addition, unlike a brig, of a gunter mast close abaft the mainmast, on which the spanker or driver was hoisted up and lowered down." Captain John Walbran's *BC Coast Names*]

Meares' first voyage was a disaster. Russian competitors had long been buying skins in Cook Inlet and Prince William Sound, and Portlock and Dixon had passed through the area just weeks before. With summer almost over, the unseasoned Meares made a fateful decision to stay the winter in Snug Corner Cove at Prince William Sound, instead of Hawaii as the Portlock expedition had done. His refuge proved anything but snug. The temperature plummeted, and the water around the ship froze allowing hundreds of curious Indigenous people to walk out to the ship. Meares was forced to fire his cannon to keep them at bay. But the dreaded scurvy proved the worst enemy. He later wrote, "Too often did I find myself called to assist in performing the dreadful office of dragging the dead bodies across the ice to a shallow sepulcher [*sic*] which our own hands had hewn out on the shore. The sledge on which we fetched our wood was their hearse, the chasms in the ice their grave." By spring, twenty-three had succumbed and only ten survived.

After this dreadful winter, Captain Dixon and the *Queen Charlotte* suddenly appeared at Snug Corner Cove. He was not amused, regarding the *Nootka* as a freeloading interloper with no right to be trading on the coast in the first place. To make matters worse, Meares and his surviving crew angered Dixon with their evasions, claiming at first to have collected two thousand pelts and then only seven hundred. Nevertheless, in concern over their wretched condition, Dixon donated stores of flour, sugar, rice, brandy and two seamen to help get the *Nootka* to Hawaii. When Captain Portlock appeared in the sound with the *King George*, he took an even harder line, demanding that Meares post a bond of £500 and agree to immediately sail for Hawaii, which he did. Although Dixon and Meares never met again, it was evident that the two men had taken an immediate dislike for each other, which found its voice in the personal accounts of their voyages.

In *A Voyage Around the World* (1789), Dixon placed the blame for the Nootka tragedy squarely on Meares. "We were informed that a free and unrestrained use of spirits had been indiscriminately allowed them [the crew] during the extreme cold weather, which they had drunk to such excess about Christmas, that numbers kept to their hammocks for a fortnight together." The liquor was of a "very pernicious kind" which was "not less fatal than the scurvy itself. It surely was ill-judged of Captain Meares to suffer such hurtful excess amongst his people."

Meares countered a year later in his book, *Voyages Made in the Years 1788 and 1789 from China to the North West Coast of America*, that Dixon's crew also suffered from the ravages of scurvy and alcoholism. "I have equal right to retaliate the same accusation upon him." This exchange set off a flurry of bitter broadside pamphlets by the two men, which form a singular footnote in West Coast history. Each accused the other of every crime in the book: falsely claiming to have discovered places found by others, selling guns to the First Nations, misappropriating place names, incompetence and greed.

In his *Remarks on the Voyage of John Meares Esq.*, Dixon retorted, "Your pompous publication is scarcely anything more than a confused heap of contradictions and misrepresentation." This demanded a response. In *An Answer to Mr. George Dixon*, Meares claimed he was only responding "that my silence not be interpreted as an acquisition in the folly of your observation and the falsehood of your assertions. I have stripped the silly jay

[Dixon] of his borrowed plumage." The last, *Further Remarks on the Voyages of John Meares Esq.*, appeared in February 1791. Dixon archly observed, "Having now pointed out a few more inconsistencies in your volume, not to call them by a harder name—I shall proceed to notice the petty malevolent assertions which fill your pamphlet." And so it went, with vicious charge and counter charge.

What are we to make of this silly squabble? Both of these men were highly skilled mariners who played major roles in BC's coastal history. Dixon "discovered" the Queen Charlotte Islands (Haida Gwaii) in 1787; and in 1790, Meares helped precipitate the famous Nootka Crisis, a political struggle for control of the north coast that brought England and Spain to the brink of war. Both are remembered by well-known BC place names today: Meares Island and Dixon Entrance. Most of the accusations seem petty and unconvincing, though Meares was the greater blowhard. An interesting question arises. How could these men of modest means afford to pay for their tedious tirades? The answer lies in economics and politics rather than ego and emotion. Both captains had the ear of the British Admiralty and business leaders. The well-informed had come to realize that our West Coast offered enormous potential, both strategically and commercially. Who knew what further treasures lurked near those rugged shores—gold? timber? fish? Russia, Spain, America and Britain all had a strong interest in the region. Which one would be the first to plant their flag? This spat was funded by third parties with little personal concern for either Meares or Dixon. Strife creates drama, which draws attention. Both government and business wanted desperately to focus public interest on this important region, and keep it in the public eye. The sea otter boom was only the beginning and Britain needed to protect her future interests.

THE STRANGE STORY
OF THE PIG WAR

Every year, San Juan Islanders stage a festival to com-
memorate the war that never was. But few realize just how
close this farcical dispute came to changing history.

Few wars have ever been waged without a single fatality yet that is exactly what happened in 1859, during a potentially nasty border dispute between the Americans and the British over San Juan Island. And
although many at the time thought it ludicrous that a war might be fought
over a pig, the root causes of the quarrel were not trivial. Indeed, they had
been festering since the signing of the Oregon Boundary Treaty of 1846.

That treaty set the long-disputed national boundary between western Canada and the US on the 49th parallel, except for Vancouver Island,
which was to remain wholly in Canada. The issue was where the boundary line would lie in the waters off Vancouver Island. The treaty itself
referred vaguely to "the middle of the channel which separates the continent from Vancouver's Island." But a quick glance at the chart shows no
fewer than three distinct channels: Rosario Strait, the San Juan Channel
and Haro Strait. Separating these channels are the three largest islands of
San Juan Group: San Juan, Orcas and Lopez. Almost immediately the du-
bious wording of the treaty started causing problems. Between 1851 and
1863, James Douglas, governor of Vancouver Island (and from 1858, all
of BC) ruled the colony like a monarch. Resolute and vigorously partisan
toward Britain and the Hudson's Bay Company (HBC), Douglas moved
quickly to establish a presence on the contested islands by granting timber
and fishing leases. By 1853 the HBC had thirteen hundred sheep on San
Juan Island, tended by a band of Hawaiian Kanaka shepherds under the
direction of Charles Griffin. A number of almost comical confrontations
followed when American customs officials arrived on the island and demanded duties from the "unlawfully imported" sheep.

Matters reached a head when US Whatcom County Sheriff Ellis
"Yankee" Barnes was dispatched to assess HBC land and collect taxes on
it. Griffin haughtily refused to pay, so Sheriff Barnes led a daring midnight raid to the island in an effort to seize Griffin's sheep for back taxes.
The venture turned into a fiasco. Halfway through the formidable task
of loading the rebellious sheep onto a barge in the dark, Griffin descend-

ed on the sheriff's posse with twenty shrieking Kanakas brandishing long knives. When the Americans drew their revolvers, the shepherds retreated, but in the confusion the terrified sheep bolted. Meanwhile, Barnes had overlooked the falling tide, and the rest of the night was spent high and dry attempting to pry the barge free and round up their lost charges. At daybreak a smudge of smoke on the horizon falsely convinced the rattled Americans that the HBC steamship *Beaver* was hot on their trail. Only thirty-four sheep were apprehended.

Governor Douglas was outraged by the armed invasion. He sent a staggering bill to the US that included the cost of the sheep, damages, overtime pay for the Kanakas, incidental losses, and the extravagant cost of hiring the *Beaver* to protect Griffin Bay from foreign attack.

Two months later, news of the squabble finally reached Washington, DC. President Franklin Pierce had little interest in a war with the British over anything, so he instructed Washington State's governor, Isaac Stevens, that territorial officials were to "abstain from all acts on the disputed grounds which are calculated to provoke any conflicts"; though at the same time, the British were not to have "exclusive rights over the premises."

A sudden wave of Indigenous unrest to the Pacific Northwest coast occurred in 1856. Governor Stevens called for help, but the US had no sizeable military force in the Northwest at the time. That, however, would soon change. Despite past disagreements, James Douglas in Victoria was quick to aid the beleaguered Americans. He supplied them with ammunition, military supplies and ordered the HBC steamships *Beaver* and *Otter* to patrol territorial waters. The assistance of the two well-armed ships turned the tide, and in due time the US Navy troop steamer *Massachusetts* arrived with two companies of troops. Commanding this expedition was Brigadier General William Selby Harney, a distinguished-looking soldier who was much given to heroic poses. Although he was an excellent horseman, his competence as a brigadier general was questionable; expressions like "manifest incapacity" and "extreme imbecility" were frequently used by fellow officers to describe him.

Gold discoveries along the Fraser River in 1858 drew hordes of seekers to BC. Perhaps as many as a hundred thousand Americans entered the colony during the period. Very quickly these new arrivals outnumbered the small HBC sheep colony on San Juan Island. Washington authorities began to issue land grants to American families living on the island to encourage further settlement. In June 1859, one of these new settlers, Lyman Cutler, was gazing over his domain when he noticed a large black pig rooting about in his prized potato garden. Impulsively, he snatched up his rifle and felled the hog with a single shot. Unfortunately the pig belonged to the

HBC. When Cutler approached Griffin and offered to make restitution, Griffin angrily demanded $100, ten times the value of the pig, and Cutler stormed out, indignant. At this delicate moment, the *Beaver* happened to steam into Griffin Bay on routine patrol with Alexander Dallas, HBC director, aboard. Griffin and Dallas confronted Cutler that afternoon, and what had started as a minor dispute between two men escalated, leading to threats of arrest from the British, and threats of violence from Cutler. In a flash, old territorial enmities returned to full boil.

General Harney soon arrived in Victoria for talks with Governor Douglas on a variety of pressing issues including the San Juan Island dispute. On the surface, everything seemed amiable enough, but some perspective on the general's true intentions were evident in this message sent to his commander-in-chief: "The population of British Columbia is largely American and foreigners; comparatively few persons from the British Isles emigrate to this region. The English cannot colonize successfully so near our people; they are too exacting. This, with the pressing necessities of our commerce on this coast will induce them to yield eventually Vancouver's Island to our government. It is as important to the Pacific States as Cuba is to those on the Atlantic."

On his return, General Harney urged American San Juan residents to present him with a petition asking for US military occupation of the island as protection against Indigenous attack. They agreed. On July 27, the *Massachusetts* landed US Army Captain George E. Pickett in Griffin Bay with sixty soldiers and three light field pieces. A fortified camp was erected and a proclamation posted asking all "Indian intrusions" to be reported to Pickett. In addition, San Juan Island was declared US territory, and no other laws or courts would be allowed on the island.

In Victoria, Governor Douglas responded by ordering a surprisingly powerful British naval force to San Juan Island. Within a few days the steam frigate *Tribune*, the gunboat *Plumper* and the steam corvette *Satellite* arrived in Griffin Bay. The steam corvette *Pylades* arrived soon after. While Pickett sweated, the British appointed Major John Fitzroy de Courcy of the *Satellite* as San Juan Island's Justice of the Peace. Major de Courcy made several spirited attempts to arrest the "pig murderer," but Cutler headed for the hills. A farcical atmosphere was heightened by crowds of sightseers who thronged to the island to enjoy the upcoming battle. Ranking British naval officers in Griffin Bay were deeply concerned that a major war was about to erupt over a trifle. Their commander, Captain Geoffrey Phipps Hornby of the *Tribune*, together with Captain George Richards of the *Plumper*, pleaded that Governor Douglas not do anything that might precipitate hostilities. However, Douglas flatly refused to back down, and Hornby was to land his marines on the island no later than August 4.

On the evening of August 3, Captain Hornby called in person at the American camp. He informed Pickett of his orders, and suggested that both forces could peacefully occupy the island as a compromise. Pickett replied that sadly this would be impos-

The gunboat *Plumper* in 1848. Ten years later the *Plumper* along with the steamboat *Corvette* and steam frigate *Tribune* arrived in Griffin Bay. Image credit: 2BJY86K Alamy

sible as he had been ordered to resist any landing by British forces, and was prepared to fight an invasion to the last man. Captain Hornby was in a quandary. If he obeyed Douglas's orders, war was certain. But he also had strong suspicions that General Harney was acting outside his authority, and had further doubts about Governor Douglas's inflexible stand. The best course seemed to play for time by disobeying orders and delaying the landing of his marines.

Harney was delighted. Obviously the British were backing down. Additional supplies and troops were off-loaded by the Americans. More ominously, Harney covertly began to recruit several hundred Americans living on Vancouver Island to come to Pickett's aid when fighting broke out. Even if these volunteers never left home, their presence "behind the lines" would certainly have put the colony at a severe disadvantage. Governor Douglas must have felt his position was very shaky, because he seriously considered a scheme to arm fifty thousand BC Indigenous men for a possible guerrilla war against the Americans on Vancouver Island.

At this critical stage, Rear Admiral Robert L. Baynes sailed into Esquimalt aboard HMS *Ganges* on routine patrol. His authority exceeded even that of Governor Douglas, and he quickly countermanded Douglas's orders to land marines on San Juan Island. In Washington DC, news of an impending war over a pig on a rock pile was met with dismay. The American Secretary of War posted a sharp letter to Harney agreeing the island was American territory but deploring the unauthorized military occupation. Harney was asked to formally explain himself, and the aged commander-in-chief of the army, General Winfield Scott, was sent to straighten the mess out.

In late October, the two generals met aboard the mail steamer *Northerner*. Scott delivered a tongue lashing that Harney never forgot. Yet when Scott demanded a voluntary resignation, Harney refused. Support for the rogue general remained very strong in the Washington territory and a demotion or court martial was out of the question. Scott moved on his own to end the crisis. He suggested to Governor Douglas a joint occupation of San Juan Island with one hundred soldiers from each side. Douglas suggested a return to the status quo with no troops on the island. Scott countered by removing all US troops and guns except for a lightly armed company of about a hundred. It was a brilliant move. War was averted, American goodwill was amply demonstrated and Douglas had little choice but to recall the warships and to land his own hundred troops for a joint occupation until a final settlement could be reached. On March 27, 1860, one hundred British marines were landed at Garrison Bay near present-day Roche Harbor. In short order, the two military camps became very friendly.

The American Civil War (1861–65) ended all discussion of this now minor border spat. Relations between the two countries remained cool during the war and for several years thereafter. This was due in large part to Britain's irritating practice of building and outfitting Confederate privateers and blockade runners to harry northern shipping during the conflict.

At last in 1871, after a joint commission failed to reach a compromise, the San Juan matter was turned over to—of all people—Kaiser Wilhem I of Germany for binding arbitration. The Kaiser, Bismark and several distinguished judicial experts were just as confused as everyone else. Most of the disputed claims were based on inaccurate maps and the conflicting ship's logs of the great 18th-century explorers. Nevertheless, it was high time the issue was laid to rest, so the Germans reluctantly awarded San Juan Island to the US and placed the boundary down the middle of Haro Strait where it remains today. Within three months the last of the British marines had left San Juan Island forever.

What would have happened if actual fighting had broken out in Griffin Bay that day in 1859? The American shore party would have been quickly evicted from their fortified camp by the British naval guns, but the subsequent war on land would have been much harder to call. Would the hundreds of Americans living on Vancouver Island and the mainland have remained neutral? Was Britain prepared to fight a protracted guerrilla war in the Northwest?

Conspiracy buffs love the Pig War. Much has been made of the fact that Harney, Pickett and some of the others involved were Southerners. Perhaps they were all working in concert to deliberately provoke a war with the British? In theory, had a major war between the two nations broken out, the North and South would have forgotten their differences to turn on their traditional enemy, England, thus avoiding the Civil War.

Another popular theory held that the Southerners were pushing for a war with England, but in hopes of a humiliating defeat for the States. Afterward, a greatly weakened US would be powerless to stop the south from seceding from the Union. Then there was the possibility of a formal military alliance between the Southern Confederacy and Britain, which would have spelled certain defeat for the Yankee North. Certainly a real Pig War would have changed history, and the map of North America might look very different today if Captain Hornby had followed orders.

Part 2

FORGOTTEN EVENTS

The Wrath of Typhoon Frieda

The story of the devastating Typhoon Frieda is a warning to future generations. The flooding of lots of cropland and destruction of houses are all in our future. Just because it hasn't happened yet doesn't mean we are invulnerable. Fierce temperature changes caused by global warming are inevitable. Frieda is relatively unknown these days but anyone who went through it remembers it vividly, yet people are still building houses in vulnerable areas.

When I arrived on Lasqueti in the spring of 1972, the island seemed pretty easygoing. With a few exceptions, none of the newly arrived hippies owned anything more than the clothes they wore and the food they ate. And living quarters were readily available for any creative squatter. With a box of nails and roll of plastic you could erect a driftwood palace almost anywhere. Large quantities of salvageable milled lumber, planks and cedar shake bolts seemed to magically wash in with every passing southeast storm. Or, if that was too much trouble, just move into one of the many empty houses and shacks that dotted the sparsely populated island.

I had always wanted to live on the water, and a friend suggested we take a look at Windy Bay on the south end. With a wide, wild, gorgeous southeast exposure facing down the Salish Sea, the bay seemed perfect. Young alder and ancient Douglas firs were bent and twisted by the wind, and the beach was a mass of small pebbles ground down by the endless surf. The fishing was grand, and there were oysters in the adjoining bay. Best of all, a half completed A-frame dwelling only needed a piece of plastic and a few 2x4s to make it liveable. Our communal party of five immediately moved in, and we lived there in cozy disharmony for several months. After a while the other couple split, but I remained there for eleven years.

Yet, for all that time there was a certain dissonance—something just did not seem quite right about the place. The quaint four-metre-square beach shack was built way above the tide line on what our friends called "logging debris"—a jumble of huge stumps, broken timber, and moss-covered bark. But Windy Bay had been largely left alone by the loggers; the wood was too twisted and warped by the ravaging winds. And then there were the piles of shattered flotsam perched almost a hundred feet above on a nearby cliff face. How could this have happened? It was only after I left years later that it became clear that I had been looking at the rapidly vanishing remnants of a huge tempest that had smashed into the bay years before.

In fact, after a little digging, I quickly discovered that the Pacific Northwest had been savaged by just such a storm on October 12, 1962, a decade before our arrival. It came unpredicted by forecasters, and seemingly unprecedented in its violence. Some in the States described this blow as the worst west coast disaster since the San Francisco earthquake, and it is still commemorated today in some parts of Washington and Oregon states. Although often referred to as "Hurricane" or "Typhoon" Frieda, it was neither.

Instead of forming over warm southern waters like these tropical disturbances, Frieda was an "extra tropical storm" or "mid-latitude cyclone." It originated in the first week of October 1962 as a tropical typhoon off Wake Island, but by October 10 had dissipated and almost disappeared. Then, in the mid-Pacific, the warm zephyrs of this minor disturbance clashed with an unusually cold airstream from the Gulf of Alaska, creating the perfect conditions for a monster storm.

Three storm surges struck the West Coast between California and British Columbia on the successive days of October 10, 11 and 12. The first was relatively weak, the second produced gale-force winds of 60 knots, and the last generated the region's worst blow in recorded history.

As this third wave approached the California coast, the storm low deepened and began to veer north. Weather prediction has grown increasingly sophisticated since 1950 with steady improvements in the great triad of weather forecasting tools: satellite imaging, radar and high-speed computers. Back in 1962, however, these systems were in their infancy and Frieda burst upon the coast with almost no warning. The first evidence that something unusual was in the works was a report from a US Navy weather ship 340 miles off the California coast on the morning of October 12. Winds were gusting to 92 knots and barometric pressure had fallen an incredible 1.7 cm in just three hours. These extreme figures were simply impossible to believe and were ignored—at first.

Shortly before noon the storm made landfall in the San Francisco Bay area. A torrential eight inches of rain caused flooding, which was followed by raging winds as high as 121 mph. Over the next twelve hours Frieda blasted north striking California, Oregon, Washington and British Columbia in rapid succession. Unlike our more traditional blows, this one moved very rapidly, cutting a narrow corridor of destruction only 200 km wide along a 1,600-km stretch. Its duration over any one area was only two hours. And Frieda was fickle, completely levelling some areas with a wrenching, twisting wind, while leaving others nearby unscathed. Although rain accompanied the storm on its devastating path, the amount of precipitation declined as it slid farther north. Barometric pressures fell to record lows all along the coast, confounding weather forecasters. Interestingly, animals like dogs, cats and cows all showed increased restlessness and agitation as Frieda drew closer.

The devastation caused by this weather event was unlike anything ever seen in the Pacific Northwest. In California, thirteen were killed, Oregon lost forty-six, Washington eleven and British Columbia seven, for a total of seventy-seven. The winds in Corvallis, Oregon, hit 125 mph, Portland 116 mph, the Columbia River Bar 150 mph, Mount Hebo radar Station 170 mph, Seattle 85 mph, Bellingham 98 mph, and the Salish Sea 148 km/h. Eleven billion board feet of timber was blown over, private home damage exceeded $210 million, and huge ocean-going ships were ripped from their moorings like toys. Millions of homes were without phones or electricity for several days, and the impassable roads were cluttered with debris and downed power lines.

By the time Frieda reached British Columbia she was weakening, but still had a vicious sting. On the afternoon of the twelfth, the waters of Victoria and Vancouver were ruffled by a light northwesterly breeze and misty drizzle. The day's forecast called for cloudiness and showers with a small craft warning and southeast winds of 25 knots. Few were aware of the devastation to the south, and many were preparing for a typical Friday night on the town. As afternoon turned into night, the wind began to pick up, and by midnight Victoria was facing sustained winds of 89 km/h with gusts to 145 km/h. In Vancouver it was much the same story with winds gusting close to 130. As a teenager in Vancouver, Randy Taylor remembers being fully supported while leaning into the howling wind.

At the height of the storm observers reported an "eerie light on the water and all through the woods, which was as bright as the early dawn." Weird electrical displays are not unusual during violent windstorms and tornadoes. Fortunately there were few small boats about at such a late hour, but a large BC Ferries ship was forced to take refuge behind Bowen Island, and the Lions Gate Bridge was shut down for the night as it swung, twisted and vibrated in the intense wind. Towboats as far north as Campbell River reported a terrifying night. Stanley Park lost hundreds of old-growth trees, and a dozen small planes were demolished along with a 42-ton Martin Mars water bomber. Power, transport and communication all crashed, and weekenders found themselves marooned far from home.

Damage in British Columbia was estimated at $10.5 million, an enormous sum in 1962.

Mercifully, after two hours Frieda began to weaken. Pressures rose and the storm divided, with one surge continuing up the West Coast and the other moving into the interior toward Hope. By 3:00 a.m. the rain had ceased and the winds died as rapidly as they had risen. As evidence of Frieda's narrow path, a fisherman friend who was anchored in the West Coast's Barkley Sound that night reported that the seas never went beyond flat calm with a typical West Coast winter drizzle. He was amazed when he heard the news the next day.

On Lasqueti the storm reached its peak around midnight, at over 78 knots (145 km/h). The winds were from the southeast, so it was the south end that bore the brunt of the storm. Today there are few who remain that remember the ferocious tempest. Ten-year-old Jan Darwin was woken up in the middle of the night as most of the roof of the Boat Cove house he was in was blown onto a nearby pickup truck. A fish boat anchored in the bay was in danger of being swamped, and his mother, Betty Darwin, was forced to brave the frigid waters to swim out to bail it and secure the lines. Even with the low tide, debris slammed against the house way above the high-water line. Hundreds of massive old-growth trees were brought down, blocking the roads and cutting the phone lines for days.

Squitty Bay was particularly hard hit. The road was washed out at the head of the bay and the log float separated from the boat ramp. False Bay was flooded, but the houses were mostly above the raging waters. Surprisingly, there were no injuries, and little damage in less exposed areas. At the time there were only a few dozen residents still living on the island, and this clearly mitigated the effects of the storm. High winds continued to lash Lasqueti for several days, hampering repairs and paralyzing communications.

Like many natural disasters, this storm spawned its share of freakish stories. In View Royal near Victoria, a carport with a large fibreglass boat suspended from the ceiling was ripped off its foundations and carried, boat and all, over the house to crash into a neighbour's bedroom. Several unwary boat owners out checking their vessels suddenly found themselves pulled helplessly into the raging storm. Miraculously all survived, although one man was in the frigid waters off Port Moody for over ninety minutes before being rescued. At Fulford Harbour, the motor launch *Big Toot* was torn from the dock and sucked into the darkness. Searchers held out little hope for recovery. One described, "At times I could hardly walk and had to turn my back on the wind. Trees were cracking and falling, and the sea was awful." At dawn the next day though, providence smiled, and the *Toot* was found safe on a nearby beach with nary a plank out of place. As a bonus, the owner also collected a 5.5-kg coho salmon trapped in the shallows by the storm.

All in all, damage from Frieda was surprisingly light in BC. Most of the seven fatalities were the result of heart attacks and electrocution from downed wires rather than wind or rain. With gusts approaching 160 km/h, there should have been a storm surge in the Salish Sea of 1.5 to 1.8 metres. Waves driven by these terrific winds should have wrecked docks and boats, flooded low-lying areas, and closed roads. The rotted debris thrown up on the cliff face above my Lasqueti cabin testified to the fierce violence of Frieda, but our coast was spared a major disaster. Why?

Blind good luck with the tides had a lot to do with it. When the storm was at its height between 11:00 p.m. and 1:00 a.m., the tide was at about 1.2 metres, so low that one could have gathered clams. This was the lowest part of the day's tidal cycle. If Frieda had arrived at 5:27 p.m. when the waters were at 4.2 metres, the story would have been very, very different. Perhaps another factor was the speed of Frieda's passage. The highest winds lasted only a couple of hours—too short a time for the seas to build to their full potential.

An important question arises at this stage in our story. Could such a powerful mid-latitude cyclone strike us again? Frieda was certainly an unusual storm. Within hours of her departure forecasters rushed to reassure the public that such an oddity could never be repeated, and so far they are right. When I originally started working on this story for *Pacific Yachting*, weather experts at Environment Canada took pains to play down the possibility of a repeat performance in the near future. They further noted that improvements in satellites, computers and radar would give forecasters a much earlier warning. But would a 24-hour advance warning make much of a difference with a storm of this magnitude? People and boats can be moved but roads, docks and buildings cannot.

And times are changing. Global warming, and the stronger El Niño events it causes are significantly altering today's weather patterns. Temperatures are up all over the Pacific, and some of these warm pools have come surprisingly close to home. "Warm blobs" off the coast of BC are becoming more frequent. Rising water levels also increase vulnerability. Warmer tropical water is being forced farther and farther east, dragging in more storms to impact on the West Coast. In October 2015 we saw the "once in a lifetime" Hurricane Oho hit northern BC. Is it only a matter of time before another Frieda barges onto our coast?

Certainly, permitting the construction of exposed homes so close to the high tide line in places like French Creek on Vancouver Island is an invitation to disaster. The immense profits and taxes to be collected from these kinds of irresponsible developments seem to have blinded planners, developers, local government and homeowners alike. And when that super storm finally does strike, it will likely be the taxpayer who foots the bill and bails out devastated homeowners.

A history of north Pacific storms would make for interesting and educational reading. There are tantalizing rumours and accounts of other big blows in Indigenous legends and in recent history, tremendous thumpers in 1880 and October 1934, in particular. But the data is sparse. With the exception of Victoria, the province only began to keep detailed weather records in 1937. Other than piles of rotting wood washed high above the tide line, monster storms leave few traces.

ADRIFT IN THE DAYS BEFORE RADIO

The sea can be cruel and unforgiving. Today even a simple cell phone would prevent many such disasters. I was particularly struck by the crass display of skeletons as told in this story.

Before the advent of ship-to-shore radio, disabled steamers were often doomed to drift helplessly in capricious north Pacific currents, while the souls aboard faced almost certain death. Today, with instant radio communication and air/sea rescue, we give little thought to a dilemma that bedevilled west coast seamen less than a century ago. What did you do when your state-of-the-art steamship broke down somewhere in the vast Pacific Ocean in the days before radio? The crew of a disabled sailing vessel could usually rig up some form of sail and limp to port, but steamships were virtually helpless.

As the 19th century progressed into the 20th, the graceful lines of sailing ships were increasingly replaced by the squat, ungainly shapes of powered hulls, ugly but capable of carrying huge cargoes. Ship-to-shore radio did not come into common use until the First World War. Being trapped aboard a derelict vessel, voiceless and perhaps just a few miles from shore, was dangerous and terrifying. Contrary winds and currents sometimes trifled with floating objects for years before casting them ashore. In the days before radio, many a ship set out and was never heard from again.

A haunting handful of these mysteries were solved months or even years after the hapless ship originally left port. In one case, the little steamship *Dora*, 293 gross tons, was engaged in carrying passengers and freight to outlying areas of western Alaska for the Northwestern Steamship Company. On December 5, 1906, it departed Kodiak for Sitka with sixteen crew and three passengers—and vanished. As the weeks went by without word, relatives and owners eventually gave up hope. Funerals were held, a new ship placed on the run, and the steamship company applied to collect the insurance from Lloyd's of London.

Then, in late February, some fifty-seven days after the *Dora* left Kodiak, the company office in Seattle received an electrifying phone call. The missing ship had finally arrived at Port Angeles, Washington, not Sitka. All aboard were emaciated and thirsty but, remarkably, still alive. Captain

Zimro Moore had a hair-raising tale to tell. Shortly after leaving Kodiak, the *Dora* was caught in one of those epic December storms for which the north Pacific is infamous. Ice built up on the topsides causing the ship to drift out of control. Within days the *Dora* was 2,000 miles off course with only twenty-four hours' worth of coal remaining in the bunkers, having been scheduled to take on more fuel at the next coastal stop.

Over the next two months the stricken *Dora* floated first south, then north, then south again—sometimes thousands of miles out at sea. At one point, Captain Moore estimated they were as far south as San Francisco. Strict rationing of food and water was imposed. Fortunately, the cargo hold contained some salt pork and flour destined for Alaska sourdoughs. The crew collected rainwater in tarps and used seawater for cooking. Moore noted that it was the driest Northwest winter he'd ever seen, and his resourcefulness undoubtedly saved them all. An inefficient sail was laboriously jury-rigged, and after several weeks the little steamship found itself off Cape Flattery. At this point, the remaining coal dust was swept from the bunkers, and the ship proceeded triumphantly into Port Angeles under its own power.

Moore was quick to point out that had the same storm caught them on the return run to Kodiak the story would have had a very different ending, because there would have been many more passengers aboard and no extra food in the hold. It's a pity no one kept a journal of the voyage because it would have made an instant bestseller.

In December of 1906, the *Dora*, along with sixteen crew and three passengers, would vanish in the frigid waters off Alaska. Image credit: Alaska Steamship Company's steamer DORA, ca. 1912, courtesy the Picture Art Collection via Alamy

The fates were not finished with Captain Moore. On a very foggy morning, August 23, 1914, he was passing Point No Point on Vancouver Island, skippering another small steamship, the *Admiral Sampson*. He was bound for Alaska with fifty-seven passengers and a heavy cargo aboard. The much larger CPR steamer *Princess Victoria* was proceeding on its scheduled route from Victoria to Seattle when they collided, ripping the smaller ship open for three-quarters of its length. Oil from ruptured fuel tanks poured out onto the sea, starting a small fire and coating the victims struggling in the water. The *Admiral Sampson*'s pumps were overwhelmed and the ship went down in just ten minutes. Fortunately, the *Princess Victoria* kept its engine turning slowly during those crucial minutes, holding the vessels locked together and keeping the *Sampson* afloat as long as possible. To the end, Moore remained on deck, supervising the evacuation. He was lost, along with sixteen others, but the professionalism of both captains undoubtedly saved many lives.

The *Centennial*, a steel-hulled paddlewheeler built in 1859, survived the American Civil War and was brought to the West Coast for the Alaska gold rush. In 1906, it departed Japan with a load of sulphur, but of course, no radio. When it failed to arrive in San Francisco after several months it was assumed that the sulphur had somehow ignited at sea and the ship had sunk with all hands.

Seven years later, in 1913, a Russian expedition exploring the Sea of Okhotsk came across a large ship with a "clipper hull" totally encased in ice. It was impossible to get aboard or even read the nameplate, but the English pilot on the Russian vessel, Captain E. Hieber, made detailed notes about the distinctive wreck. Upon his return, the ship was positively identified as the *Centennial*. Its normal course would have brought it close to the Kuril Islands and the southern entrance to the Sea of Okhotsk. Most likely it had suffered a mechanical failure and been trapped by ice. Charts of the time showed a small Russian trading post nearby, and it's likely the crew attempted to reach it by walking across the ice. Sadly, the outpost had long since been abandoned, and they vanished without a trace. It's possible the *Centennial* is still entombed and afloat, but more likely it was crushed and sunk long ago.

This final story took place long after most ships were required by law to carry radio equipment. Nevertheless, some poorer operators could not (and still cannot) afford this luxury. On Halloween 1927, the Japanese fishing sampan *Ryo Yei Maru* was found drifting off Cape Flattery. Apparently deserted, the 60-foot hull was encrusted with barnacles, and long strands of seaweed festooned its sides. The boarding party was greeted by a fearful sight: a deck littered with human bones, and the master mummified in his cabin.

The *Ryo Yei Maru*'s log showed it had departed Misaki, Japan, with a crew of twelve on December 5, 1926. The engine soon broke down and the ship drifted until December 23 when it encountered the steamer *West Ison* bound for San Francisco. Captain Richard Healy begged the itinerant fishermen to abandon their disabled craft and come aboard, but they refused. Understandably the fishermen faced a cruel dilemma: they could save themselves but lose their ship and livelihood. They gambled that good luck, favourable drift and perhaps a tow might get them safely to port… and they lost.

The story did not end there. After its 5,000-mile drift, the *Ryo Yei Maru* was towed into Seattle. Curious gawkers soon gave promoters the bizarre idea of putting the boat and its grisly cargo on display as a tourist attraction. When the Japanese owners and families at home got wind of the scheme, they were understandably horrified. The sampan was promptly hauled out and burned, and the crew's remains cremated. Services were held at the Buddhist Temple in Seattle.

There are many who decry the proliferation of modern "toys" we take to sea these days: radar, GPS, fish finders, generators, various types of radios, even cell phones near shore. But radio communication is vital. And let the modern traveller beware. Some commercial vessels in the developing world still lack working radios. Mishaps on crowded ferries in the Philippines, Thailand and Indonesia were far more deadly than they might have been because help was not summoned promptly.

RUMRUNNER MEMORIES

Not only did American prohibition spawn a race between Canadian smugglers and the cops, it set off a technological competition to see who could build the fastest boat. Signs of the struggle can be found in caches of liquor bottles and the stories of a few old men who remain from those days. I had a chance to interview a ninety-year-old wireless operator from one of the mother ships off the British Columbia coast and from a well-respected old British Columbia family, but at the last minute the meeting was cancelled by the relatives for fear of scandal. Such is life for a journalist.

The square antique bottle lay half buried in the sand, an embossed side poking just above the surface. "Champion Concentrated Embalming Fluid, Springfield Ohio, Complies With All State Laws." A finely graduated scale in ounces had been thoughtfully provided on the side of the bottle. It seemed a perfect find. I carefully placed it in my pack and returned to the ruined homestead.

We had been slowly motoring our way along the coast of the northern Gulf Islands when we noticed a glint among the trees. The founda-

The *Malahat* was a large ship typical of the "mother ships" that waited offshore to be loaded by the smaller rumrunner boats. It could carry up to 10,000 crates of bootleg. Image credit: Malahat CVA447 2426

tions of a crude shelter, now collapsed, lay in a clearing, crowned by a large pile of greenish scrap metal and piping. A shimmering pile of broken glass littered one side of the narrow beach where hundreds of bottles had been broken by someone with nothing better to do. Strangely, they were all the same embalming fluid bottles. Who could have been using so much of the stuff? This isolated bay with no road access certainly seemed a peculiar place for a mortuary.

Several weeks later while sharing a brew with some local old-timers I told them about my find. They laughed knowingly, "There's some that used to drink that stuff."

"What?!" I said. "Get serious. Embalming fluid is deadly poison."

"Yes and no," they replied. "Those bottles probably contained some of the better moonshine produced on this coast. What better way to flummox the police than to pass their stuff off as embalming fluid?"

It turns out that I had happened on a genuine archaeological site, where thousands of gallons of potent, quality alcohol were produced for smuggling into the States during the American liquor prohibition of 1919–33. Even beer was forbidden then, although small amounts of wine and beer could be legally brewed and consumed in the home. The value of a

Canadian prohibition lasted only briefly during World War I. Although taken in 1890, this picture of a bar in a tree celebrates the spirit of speakeasy culture during the USA prohibition. Image credit: Major James Skitt Matthews (1878-1970), City of Vancouver Archives, AM54-S4-: St Pk P34

case of fine Canadian whisky in Seattle shot up from $25 to $250 overnight.

During the First World War, both the provincial and the federal governments tried to enforce their own liquor prohibition, but the effort was a fiasco. Bootlegging became rife, the police were corrupted, and people just kept drinking. Washing their hands of the mess, Ottawa bureaucrats decided to leave the liquor question up to the provinces, and BC became one of the first to allow the sale of packaged liquor from government stores in 1920. Thus was born a golden opportunity for anyone with a taste for adventure and a boat.

At first the business was haphazard and disorganized. Anyone with a dinghy could pick up a few bottles at the liquor store, wait for a moonless night, and sail over for delivery to the American Gulf Islands or Puget Sound. The US Coast Guard quickly became aware of these amateur intrusions and beefed up patrols in vulnerable areas such as the Juan de Fuca and Haro Straits. But smuggling was too profitable to abandon, and a technological race soon exploded between rumrunners and American authorities. The dynamics of the game were simple. The fastest boat won the day. If you could outrun the Yankee cops, you were home free with a comfortable wad of cash in your pocket.

The Canadian liquor smugglers enjoyed two huge advantages. The first was local expertise in advanced motorboat design. North America had been on the cutting edge of speedboat technology during the First World War, producing hundreds of sleek sub chasers and coastal patrol boats for the Allies. The second was the recent development and availability of low-cost, high-powered gasoline motors.

The Liberty engine was to have been America's great contribution to victory in World War I. Originally designed as an airplane engine by two of America's most gifted motorcar engineers in 1917, it went from drawing board to production in less than a year. This V-12 weighed 825 pounds and cranked out a remarkable 400 hp, giving it the best power-to-weight ratio in the world for its time. But the engine was developed too late to play a major role in hostilities, and thousands soon became available as war surplus for a few hundred dollars each. America's loss became the rumrunner's gain. Up to four of these beasts were crammed below decks in pairs, giving some of the most matronly looking of vessels a remarkable turn of speed when needed. Boats of 80 feet could make 20 knots fully loaded, and one streamlined 30-footer was clocked at almost 50 knots.

By the mid-1920s the trade had become highly organized with a dozen or more mother ships holding station on "Rum Row" off the California, Oregon and Washington coasts. American jurisdiction initially extended only three miles offshore, but this was increased late[r] miles. The most notorious of these rum ships was the *Malah[e]* long and displacing 1,500 tons. It could carry a boggling eighty-[fou]~ sand cases in its hold with an additional sixteen thousand on deck. Coded short wave radio communications emanating from a private office in Vancouver arranged for speedy shore boats to rendezvous, off-load, and run the booty to shore. They sported such names as *Zip*, *Skeezix*, *Kagome*, *Quickinish*, *Yaparongra* and *Alibi Wahoo*. Most of these vessels were powered by the legendary Liberty engines, and a few can still be found in west coast waters today.

Life aboard the waiting mother ships was not easy. Months were spent far out to sea in even the worst weather. The food was canned and monotonous, the work hard and dangerous, and the routine deadly boring. The money, however, was excellent. Deckhands made $125 a month and captains $500, with nowhere to spend it until they got back home. Despite enough booze for a thousand parties aboard, drinking was usually strictly forbidden. With that kind of pay, the organizers, mainly Vancouver businessmen, were able to man and staff their ships with the very best personnel. Crews were highly competent, experienced and honest.

To further simplify operations, the businessmen behind the rumrunners joined forces to form Consolidated Exporters, with a large warehouse operating openly on Hamilton Street in Vancouver. The company specialized in quality bonded liquor, and steered clear of illicit moonshine whenever possible. Captain Charles H. Hudson, a master smuggler himself and "marine superintendent" of Consolidated Exporters, wryly observed, "We operated perfectly legally. We considered ourselves public philanthropists! We supplied good liquor to poor thirsty Americans who were poisoning themselves with rotten moonshine. All who were employed in the business had all the excitement and thrills of a war without the risk."

Hudson knew what he was talking about. He served with distinction during both world wars. The brewers, organizers, captains and deckhands could hardly be considered "criminals" in the normal sense of the word because technically, they skirted the US laws. In reality, they saw themselves as bold entrepreneurs making money off America's foibles. Sadly, the BC rumrunners were (and still are) an extremely close-mouthed fraternity. I had a frustrating time attempting to interview aged crew members who love to talk up the good old rumrunning days with their kids and grandkids, but clam up the moment they hear the word "journalist." "Don't never tell nothin' to nobody nohow" is still the golden rule. We may be sure that the big fish at the top made out exceedingly well, but their identities and the details of their operations remain elusive.

Initially powerless to halt the traffic with their outmoded patrol boats, the American Coast Guard began to produce their own speedy rum chasers—36-footers capable of 25 knots, and 100-foot "Dollar" boats. Vessels confiscated from occasional unlucky smugglers were also pressed into service. This new breed was armed with a 3.25-inch gun forward, complemented by two Lewis machine guns. It was not uncommon for a chase to develop on the high seas, with the Americans stolidly popping away, as their wildly twisting quarry frantically dumped cases over the side. Amazingly, no one was killed during those confrontations on the West Coast, but there were fatalities on the Atlantic side. When even these stringent methods failed to stem the flow of demon alcohol, the Americans began to seize ships far outside the three-mile limit. One such was the *Quadra*, a converted lighthouse tender capable of carrying 25,000 cases. It was apprehended at gunpoint off the California coast by the Coast Guard cutter *Shawnee* in October 1925. Although more than 20 miles offshore at the time, the Quadra was towed to San Francisco and remained tied up in legal wrangles for years. The illicit cargo somehow mysteriously disappeared and, although several of the crew were sentenced to jail and fined, all jumped bail and returned to Canada. Such high-handed actions in international waters created an uproar, but it soon became apparent that the real aim of the Americans was to take the big rum ships out of service by any means necessary. Other victims included the mother ships *Coal Harbour* and *Federalship*, shelled and boarded after a long chase more than 300 miles off the California coast.

The liquor trade brought enormous prosperity to the Canadian Gulf Islands. The multitude of small, isolated coves, bays and islets between Vancouver Island and the mainland were tailor-made for clandestine activities. A remote bay on Texada was once the home of a huge three-storey operation housed in a giant, barn-like structure. The liquor was fermented using potatoes or grain, distilled in large metal vats, and then pumped via underground pipes into tanks aboard waiting vessels. Hundreds of litres were produced every month until the British Columbia Provincial Police (BCPP) shut the operation down in the early '30s.

The provincial police were at a severe disadvantage in their attempts to combat rumrunning; lax Canadian laws actually encouraged the trade. But moonshining at home remained highly illegal. Further, the enormous cash profits generated could not help but attract a criminal element. There were numerous hijackings and even occasional murders, as occurred on the *Beryl G*. Smugglers routinely carried guns, and some bolted steel plates to their hulls for additional protection. Still, the level of prohibition mayhem here never approached that of the States. The marine arm of the

BCPP attempted to curb the law-breaking, but their boats were no match for the hi-tech Liberty-powered speedsters. Guile was the best method for making an arrest. In the late '20s George Hadley of Lasqueti Island built his famous teapot house with two distinct chimneys—one shaped like a teapot and the other a sugar bowl. Hadley was adept at brewing more than tea but was careful to sell his product only to friends and trusted business partners. The man was a gifted inventor who never seemed able to turn a dime on his ideas but was able to produce a superlative grade of moonshine. One late November night there was a knock at Hadley's door. A bedraggled fisherman hauled himself in with a sad tale of a sunken boat and financial ruin. He had heard that George produced the best in the west, and just wanted one little bottle to help him through the loss. Hadley was apparently suspicious at first but the story was convincing. He finally relented, and with good wishes parted with a bottle, a serious blunder. The next day the provincial police arrived in force. Hadley was arrested for selling to an undercover "operative." His booze was confiscated, and his large still dragged down to the dock and loaded on a barge for Nanaimo. Sentenced to six months at Oakalla Penitentiary, George never returned to brewing or to Lasqueti Island.

Other rumrunning centres were D'Arcy Island in the Haro Strait and Discovery Island off Victoria. Both served as way stations where smugglers could pick up gas or supplies, wheel and deal, or just pass the time while waiting for a rendezvous. Clo-oose, north of Victoria, turned into a bustling thieves' market where all sorts of forbidden products were available including opium and stolen luxury goods.

Alas, in 1933 the liquor gravy train ran out of steam. American President Franklin D. Roosevelt threw out the hated Volsted Act, bringing an end to prohibition (and the prosperity of west coast rumrunners). The effects in coastal BC were dramatic, and because they came at the height of the Depression, it was especially painful. The rum ships returned home, paid off their crews, and moved on to less lucrative pastimes. Illicit distillers closed their doors, and abandoned equipment rusted where it lay. Many joined the unemployment lines as a colourful era of coastal history ended forever. Yet for the discerning observer, evidence of those days can still be found all around us.

THE FATHER OF THE VANCOUVER ISLAND PILOT

Unlike Captain Turner of the *Clio*, Captain Richards showed great consideration for the First Nations under his jurisdiction. His charts in the *Vancouver Island Pilot* were so accurate they were in use until quite recently. His quick thinking saved his expedition on numerous occasions.

Trincomali Channel, Malaspina Strait, Meares Island, Sabine Channel, Ganges Harbour, Denman and Hornby Islands are just a few of the hundreds of familiar BC coastal landmarks named by Captain George Henry Richards, one of the great naval surveyors of the 19th century. With "extraordinary energy and almost severe zeal," Richards conducted the first thorough examination of the waters around Vancouver Island between 1857 and 1863. The results of his work appeared as the *Vancouver Island Pilot*, which for many years remained the best guide to the area.

In the mid-1800s, a coastal survey of Vancouver Island was long overdue. No reliable charts of the shoal-bound coast existed at the time, a deficiency that greatly slowed settlement. In addition, a squabble was brewing between Britain and the US over the boundary between the two countries. Of particular concern was the disposition of San Juan Island. There was also considerable interest in the coal deposits that had recently been discovered on Vancouver Island. Steam power was rapidly replacing sail, and the strategic location of coal fields was a major concern for naval planners.

The Admiralty's choice of Captain Richards to head the survey was no surprise. Born in 1820, Richards had entered the Royal Navy at age twelve. His first break came in 1847 when he was appointed second captain of the paddle steamer *Acheron*, then surveying New Zealand. Over the next four years he did stellar work charting these difficult islands, often using small open boats. *The New Zealand Pilot*, published in 1856, set a high standard for future efforts. Although the bulk of this work was dry, no-nonsense sailing instructions, Richards had a literary flair and perceptiveness that make for interesting reading even today. "The appearance of this iron-bound coast cleft asunder as it were into harbours by some awful convulsion of nature, presents a scene truly grand and solitary; no inhabitants but the tenants of the forest, the Ka-Ka-Po and Kiwi, rare and remarkable birds known in no other country; and no single spot of level land," Richards wrote in his introduction.

Soon after returning from this challenging assignment, Richards was called upon to be second-in-command of the Assistance under Captain Edward Belcher. Belcher led a small fleet deep into the Canadian Arctic in search of the missing Franklin expedition. Although this five-ship effort turned into a fiasco when Belcher abandoned four of his vessels in the ice, Richards was absolved of blame. Indeed, he made one of the most extraordinary sledging trips on record during the voyage.

In 1856, then in his mid-thirties, Richards was sent to survey Vancouver Island. *HMS Plumper*, the ship selected for the task, proved a poor choice. A barque-rigged steam sloop displacing 484 tons, it was obsolete, cramped and rotten. An awkward room to survey charts, which pleased no one, was constructed on deck. The feeble 60 hp steam engine provided a top speed of only 6 knots. Progress was slowed by a major leak off the Bay of Biscay, followed by a broken shaft, but the ship finally arrived at Esquimalt on November 7, 1857. First on the agenda was the boundary survey. Richards and his team worked closely with the American Boundary

In 1861 Captain Richards' HMS *Hecate* ran aground in fog on a rocky islet near Cape Flattery. A rising tide set it free and the battered ship needed major repairs in San Francisco. Image credit: Courtesy of Maritime Museum of British Columbia, P1029

The HMS *Plumper* was selected for the task of surveying Vancouver Island but proved a poor choice. A barque-rigged steam sloop, it was obsolete, cramped and rotten. It's feeble 60 hp steam engine provided a top speed of only 6 knots. Image credit: A-00238, courtesy the Royal BC Museum and Archives, original sketch held by the Royal Museums Greenwich

Commission and were happy to discover that their line on the mainland at the 49th parallel agreed almost exactly with the Americans' survey. But San Juan Island proved a more vexing problem. The 1846 Oregon Boundary Treaty between the two countries referred vaguely to "the middle of the channel which separated the continent from Vancouver's Island." But a glance at the chart shows no less than three clear channels dividing the two land masses: Rosario Strait, San Juan Channel and Haro Strait. This was going to take more than a couple of survey parties to remedy, and soon blew up into a nasty confrontation between the two countries.

Over the next six years Richards and his crew visited or surveyed the entire coast of Vancouver Island, as well as parts of the Fraser River, some of the interior of Vancouver Island and the mainland. The *Plumper* was replaced in December 1860 by the *Hecate*, a paddlewheel sloop of 860 tons mounting five guns. In 1864, Richard C. Mayne, who served as lieutenant on the *Plumper* and the *Hecate*, published a vivid account of their adventures entitled *Four Years in British Columbia and Vancouver Island* (reprinted in 1969). Richards methodically visited each area for several days or weeks, then returned to Esquimalt to refit, draw up his charts, and organize his notes.

First published by the Admiralty in 1861 and repeatedly revised, *The*

Vancouver Island Pilot made sea voyages to BC a great deal less dangerous and difficult. The timing of its publication was almost perfect because gold was discovered along the Fraser in 1859. The resulting frenzy drew tens of thousands to the area. Like Richards' New Zealand effort, *The Vancouver Island Pilot* concentrated on straightforward sailing directions with an emphasis on trouble spots like Seymour Narrows, Victoria Harbour, and the west coast of the Island. It included useful information on diverse topics such as Indigenous Peoples, climate, the interior of the colony, farming, mining, and speculation on the future. Richards made a prescient colonialist observation about the Fraser River: "this magnificent stream pursues its undevious course into the Strait of Georgia; and there can be little doubt that it is destined, at no distant period, to fulfill to the utmost, as it is already partially fulfilling, the purposes for which nature ordained it—the outlet for the products of a great country, whose riches in mineral and agricultural wealth are daily being more fully discovered and developed." Of course the truth of this prediction ensured things did not work out as well for the Indigenous Peoples of British Columbia.

During his years on the coast, Richards witnessed and participated in many important events that shaped our province. His good sense, patience, and reluctance to use force set him apart from many Royal Navy gunboat captains of the time. During the summer of 1859, the simmering dispute over San Juan Island erupted into a tense armed standoff. Against orders, the ambitious American general, William Selby Harney, landed sixty troops with three light field pieces on the island to protect against intrusions by Indigenous warriors. The equally hot-headed Governor James Douglas called on the *Tribune* (31 guns), the steam corvette *Satellite* (21 guns), and Richards' *Plumper* to stand off the island and land a contingent of Royal Marines to force the issue. Captain Geoffrey Phipps Hornby of the *Tribune* and Richards refused to be swept up in the hysteria and prudently delayed until saner heads could be consulted. When Rear Admiral Robert Baynes, commander of the North Pacific Squadron, sailed into Esquimalt a few days later, his first action was to countermand Douglas's ill-conceived order. England had just fought the costly Crimean War, and the US was on the verge of its own bloody Civil War. An ugly confrontation over San Juan Island was in neither side's interest, and the "Pig War," as the affair came to be known, eventually ended peacefully.

On several other occasions, Richards and his crew were called upon to act as reinforcement for the thinly spread Royal Navy. For the rapidly arriving colonists, stability and peace were seen as essential to prosperity. Aside from aiding colonization, imposing the British system of law and order on Indigenous Peoples was an attempt to end the occurrences of tribal warfare, raiding and slavery. Illegal liquor sales and the sudden availability of firearms made these conflicts far more deadly for everyone. Richards showed unusual sympathy and understanding for Indigenous People. In December 1860 he faced a tense group of Kwagiulth at Fort Rupert on Vancouver Island. Furious over the murder of one of their chiefs by the Songhees in Victoria, they were plotting revenge. Richards argued eloquently that it would not do to take the law into their own hands; rather, the accused murderers should be tried in a court of law and executed if found guilty.

Mayne described the scene: "At this moment the brother of the murdered chief interposed, and nearly brought the meeting to a close in some confusion by jumping up and announcing his intention of going at once with all the men he could get to revenge his brother's death. This was mere bravado, however, and he was soon pacified. At last, after a great deal of violent language and action, the chiefs said they were quite willing to give up the custom of killing and making slaves, if the other tribes of the island would amend their ways also." It is worth noting that five years later a similar confrontation in this same village led to its complete destruction by Captain Edwin Brooke Turnour of the HMS *Clio*.

In a remarkable letter to Admiral Baynes on "white Indian" relations, Richards noted that wrongs were committed by both sides, but "my opinion is that the Natives in most instances are the oppressed and injured parties. The white man supplies him with intoxicating spirits under the influence of which most of these uncivilized acts are committed. The white man in too many instances considers himself entitled to demand their wives or their sisters, and if such demand is disputed, to proceed to acts of violence to gain their object."

During their frenetic five years of surveying, Richards' expedition had only one very close call. Passing Cape Flattery on a foggy morning in August 1861, the *Hecate* suddenly found itself hemmed in by a wall of crashing foam and jagged rocks. By unfortunate chance, the crew had miscalculated their entrance into Juan de Fuca Strait and cut too close to shore. The *Hecate* was driven aground on a tiny group of islands just inside the cape. A moderate northwest wind blew the ship sideways where it crashed repeatedly against the rocks, the "masts springing like whips" and the boiler spouting steam. It appeared the ship was doomed, but fortunately the tide was rising.

After "two tremendous crashes sending us flying about in different directions," the ship managed to pull free and floated, badly battered, into a narrow cove. The chief engineer reported that the cross-sleepers holding the heavy steam engine had been shattered and that one more bump would

THE "BEAVER," PIONEER STEAMER OF THE PACIFIC COAST.

The Hudson Bay Co. SS *Beaver* was the first steam powered vessel on the Salish Sea, and the first ship drawn into the Pig War. Governor Douglas tried to extract payment from the Americans for its extravagant chartering costs. Image credit: Alamy 2JF8TWW

certainly have sent the vessel to the bottom. On the return to Esquimalt, it was clear that *Hecate* was severely damaged. Close to fifty sheets of copper sheathing had been ripped off its bottom, dozens of planks broken, and the entire superstructure weakened. The ship was temporarily patched up and sent to the only floating dry dock on the West Coast, in San Francisco, where it spent two months undergoing repairs.

In December 1862, Richards and the *Hecate* were recalled to England via the South Pacific. Daniel Pender continued the BC survey in SS *Beaver*, hired from the Hudson's Bay Company for that purpose. Richards was soon appointed head of the important Department of Hydrography, a post he held for ten years. He streamlined the bureaucracy of his department, vastly increasing the number of charts it produced, and pushed vigorously for detailed ocean pilot charts that included wind and current data in addition to geographic landmarks. He also found time to survey the soon-to-be-opened Suez Canal and promote several important scientific expeditions. He was knighted, appointed a Fellow of the Royal Society, and made full admiral. The life of this extraordinary man, who died in 1900 at the age of eighty, deserves a book.

Sources:

Gough, Barry M., *Gunboat Frontier, British Maritime Authority and Northwest Coast Indians 1846–1890*. Vancouver, BC: UBC Press, 1984.

Mayne, Richard Charles, *Four Years in British Columbia and Vancouver Island*. London, UK: John Murray, 1862; S.R. Publishers Ltd., 1969.

Walbran, John T., *British Columbia Coast Names 1592–1906*. Ottawa, ON: J.J. Douglas Ltd., 1971.

THE CALAMITOUS CRUISE
OF THE *CLIO*

The Royal Navy demanded the complete subservience of the First Nations in British Columbia. The slightest sign of rebellion brought into play the most advanced weapons of the age, which included breech-loading Armstrong guns. When the people of the "Native Ranch" of Ku-kultz resisted, the village was completely destroyed. In this way Imperial colonialism was imposed on Indigenous People in British Columbia and elsewhere.

In the middle years of the 19th century, the calculating and all-seeing eyes of the British Empire focused anew on Canada's "unpopulated" Northwest coast. Aside from the obvious commercial possibilities in whale oil, seal skins, coal and lumber, there was also a desire to counter growing US influence in the area. Further, it was hoped that settlement would be encouraged if law and order were brought to this wild and remote part of the world. In particular, the authorities wished to halt the highly lucrative trade in alcohol and slaves among the Indigenous Peoples.

The concern was more than academic. Between 1858 and 1870, as many as a hundred thousand BC First Nations People may have died of alcoholism and its complications. In those Victorian days, many new settlers in the colonies of Vancouver Island and British Columbia felt a moral obligation to root out this terrible scourge. In 1854, the Colony of Vancouver Island passed laws forbidding the sale or gifts of liquor to the Indigenous People. As so often happens when regulating mind-altering substances, the best intentions can lead to an awesome exercise in folly and futility but also to the abuse of those supposedly being helped. Such was the case with the cruise of the steam corvette HMS *Clio* on routine patrol on Pacific Station late in 1865.

Clio, commanded by Captain Nicholas Edward Brooke Turnour, was on the cutting edge of the naval technology of the time. Built in 1858 and displacing 1,470 tons, the ship was fast, long and mean. The newly invented marine-screw propeller coupled to a 400 hp steam engine provided power. This radical innovation allowed the ship to patrol confined bays, rivers and estuaries where sailing vessels would never venture. *Clio*'s complement of 290 sailors and marines were well versed in amphibious landings, small

The gun deck of the HMS *Satellite*. The *Clio*'s 110 pounders were nearly twice as large as these sixty-four pounders. Image credit: National Parks Gallery, public domain

arms and, of course, handling their 110-pounder Armstrong guns.

The Armstrong naval gun was the most advanced of its time, capable of hurling a massive, high-explosive shell with terrible effect. Its rifled barrel and breech-loading mechanism made it the most accurate and quick firing in the world. Although *Clio*'s displacement rated her among the smaller of Her Majesty's warships, the combination of steam power and firepower made the ship invincible on this coast.

After departing Esquimalt on November 16, *Clio* stopped briefly at Nanaimo and then Fort Rupert on northern Vancouver Island for coal. By early December the ship had reached Metlakatla near present-day Prince Rupert. Metlakatla, founded in 1862 by the charismatic resident Anglican lay missionary William Duncan, was a curious Utopian experiment of three hundred North Coast Indigenous people. His motto was to "Instruct, delight, overcome or bend the will." Alcohol was forbidden as was traditional medicine, gambling, face painting and potlatching. Enforcement was carried out by twenty uniformed Indigenous constables—more than in all the rest of BC at the time. The value of hard work was emphasized, and the little community made ends meet by exporting furs, handicrafts, fish and lumber. All were expected to be industrious, orderly, clean, peaceful and honest. Settlers were obliged to pay a village tax, grow a garden, go to church and build a wooden house identical to all the others. They even

In 1865 the Indigenous village of Ku-Kultz at Fort Rupert had an estimated population of 1,500 before the devastation of smallpox. Image credit: Canadian Museum of History via Wikimedia Commons, public domain

had a brass band.

Captain Turnour had a tumultuous meeting with Duncan soon after his arrival. The reverend complained bitterly about flagrant violations of the liquor laws in the Indian Act by whisky sellers at nearby Fort Simpson. He begged Captain Turnour to arrest the criminals and bring them to Metlakatla for trial. Although Duncan had no legal training, his unquestionable moral stature had led to his appointment as chief magistrate of the area. The *Clio*'s captain acted decisively. A lieutenant commanding the ship's pinnace, two cutters and a launch was dispatched to Fort Simpson to enforce the law and stop the trade in "demon" alcohol.

The smuggling sloop *Eagle* was discovered at Nass in the Portland Inlet, close to the Russia-Alaska border. The vessel made a run for it but was captured along with master Knight and seaman Costello. The schooner *Nonpareil* was also seized with Captain Stevens and Sebastapol, a well-known liquor trader on the Skeena River. Large quantities of whisky were also confiscated. Four days later the *Clio*'s crew struck at Kitimat. But bad news travels fast and little liquor was found. A British participant described the scene: "We proceeded from house to house hunting up various men who were wanted in connection with the crime alleged, and who gave us much trouble from their natural desire to remain where they were. After some time, during which many high words were muttered, and as coolly answered by the significant appearance of the bright ends of bayonets and the sharp click of the rifle, and the disarming of one unlucky animal with a short musket ready loaded and cocked for the especial benefit of the First Lieutenant."

The prisoners were taken on board the *Clio* and jailed at Metlakatla. During the lengthy trials that followed several more raids were made at Fort Simpson and more whisky sellers were arrested. The white defendants received stiff sentences ranging from five to eight years in the slammer or a fine of £500–800 sterling. The Indigenous people received lesser sentences. With the trials finally over and the prisoners safely stowed on board for delivery to jail in Victoria, the *Clio* took on 102 cords of wood for the return voyage.

Up to now the cruise of the *Clio* had been purely routine. But when the ship arrived at Beaver Harbour off Fort Rupert on December 22, they found a tense, dangerous situation had developed during their absence. An Indigenous person from Newitty, 35 miles to the north, had been murdered by a group from the large village of Ku-kultz, which lay in the shadow of Fort Rupert. Hudson's Bay Company agent Pym N. Compton had prevented a series of revenge killings only by persuading the angry Newitties to wait for the return of the *Clio* and British justice. As had happened so many times before, the *Clio* lowered its boats and a landing party sped toward the village. Once on shore, a Lieutenant Carey demanded the surrender of the three murder suspects and the right to search Ku-kultz for liquor. Carey's own words best describe what happened next.

> On landing I was met on the beach by "Jim," the Chief of the Tribe, who asked for what purpose we had landed. I told him to secure the three murderers, and destroy any whisky we might find. He refused to give the natives up unless we gave him two of our men as hostages; during that time about 50 Indians assembled on the beach, and about the same number near the Ranch, armed with muskets, they commenced yelling, and fired in the air over our heads. Jim, the chief was evidently the prime mover, he appeared to be urging his men to fire on us, and was very threatening in his manner. I told him he should have a certain time to give the men up, and if they were not forthcoming, we would open fire from the ship and destroy the village.

The Indigenous men refused Carey's demands and threatened to fire on the fort and even attack the *Clio*—the latter clearly a hopeless proposition. Chief Jim and ten other inhabitants of Ku-kultz were taken prisoner and removed to the ship. The next day Captain Turnour decided to make good on his threats. The *Clio* moved closer to the village, big guns were rolled out and Ku-kultz was bombarded with 110-pound explosive shells. The inhabitants quickly sought refuge behind Fort Rupert and the marines within prudently held their fire. "We ascertained that a man and his wife were severely confused by the bursting of a shell in one of the houses. I saw a shot strike close to the man who was hoisting the white flag, but he appeared as unconcerned as possible neither looking to the right nor to the left."

The flag of truce ended the shelling and the *Clio* pulled back for the night to await developments. Of deaths or injuries the accounts say nothing. Mr. Compton and Mr. Moss, the Indian Agent, pleaded with the villagers to surrender the murderers or face the consequences. One eventually did give himself up but the other two steadfastly refused to surrender. The following morning, three boats of tars and marines landed and again their demands were flatly refused, at which point:

> nothing more was said, but to work they went, and in a very few minutes the camp was on fire. The Indians, determined to resist our demands had buried most of their valuables underground inside their houses during the night, and consequently lost most of their winter provisions.

A firebreak arrested the flames before the village was totally consumed, but the unburned cedar houses were rekindled with torches after another ultimatum met the same stout refusal.

By this time, the demand to search the ruined village could no longer be resisted and "a good quantity of rum was found and destroyed" amongst the wreckage. All that remained of Ku-kultz, once home to between fifteen hundred and three thousand people, were one hundred canoes pulled up on the beach. The marines turned their attention to them next and quickly destroyed the lot with hatchets and axes. The *Clio* seized seven hostages for good behaviour and sailed for Nanaimo arriving on Christmas Day, and Victoria soon after.

Within days of the *Clio*'s return it became apparent that Reverend Duncan's stern sentences at Metlakatla were not going to stand. On January 10, a writ of habeas corpus freed the convicted whisky sellers after they posted a shockingly low £100 bail. The prisoners from Kitimat, Port Simpson and Ku-kultz were all released without charge and told to make their way home as best they could. What happened? Colonial income from the sale of alcohol was considerable and it seems likely that many at the highest levels of government did not want to see a large part of this tax windfall suddenly dry up.

This act of indecision on the part of the colonial legal authorities raised a furor in the colony of Vancouver Island. What was the point of going to all the trouble to enforce the liquor laws when the culprits were released as soon as they arrived in Victoria? And many felt that excessive force was used when the "Indian Ranch" and canoes were completely destroyed for shooting muskets in the air and defying British orders. How was it possible to "save" the village from alcohol by completely flattening it? Although no one wanted to go on record as criticizing Captain Turnour, members of the legislative assembly began to clamour for further details about the unfortunate affair at Fort Rupert. Arthur Kennedy, the governor of Vancouver Island, stonewalled by writing to the legislature that unfortunately he had no papers on the matter and could not comment. And that was that.

Everyone lost in the confrontation at Ku-kultz. The Royal Navy was successfully defied and shown to be both incompetent and brutal. The liquor trade was fostered by governmental dilly-dallying and indecision. The colonial authorities were revealed as callous, uncaring and far more interested in hushing things up than in producing a sound and consistent alcohol policy. The inhabitants of Ku-kultz lost their homes, livelihoods and in some cases, probably life and limb as well as facing starvation from the loss of their winter provisions and canoes. And there were considerable travel expenses for those stranded in Victoria, hundreds of miles from home.

Captain Turnour's handling of this situation was not typical of all British gunboat captains on our coast. Many, like Captain George Henry Richards of HMS *Plumper* and Captain James C. Provost of HMS *Virago*, showed great tact and diplomacy in defusing similar ugly situations. Why did things go so badly for Turnour? Perhaps a contributing factor was the captain's relative inexperience in dealing with Indigenous people. He had been on the Pacific Station only a year before the incident took place. On the other hand, knowing as little as we do about Turnour's motivations, it is entirely possible that he was merely following orders from above. This incident could well have been intended as a deliberate and officially sanctioned show of brute force in a troublesome neighbourhood.

THE PACIFIC COAST
MILITIA RANGERS

FORGOTTEN DEFENDERS OF
CANADA'S WEST COAST

This story is a tale of unbridled paranoia. Enormous sums were allocated to block a possible invasion by the Japanese at the start of World War II. Jittery observers saw supposed airplanes over Vancouver and Victoria and residents of the inner coast darkened their shades at night to protect against enemy warships. Large groups of men were organized as a sort of guerrilla army to counter the threat. There are some who believe that supplies for the Japanese occupation of British Columbia still exist on our northern coast, but in the end, it was all for nothing as the Japanese never intended to invade North America.

It is hard to imagine today just how grim the war situation was for Canada in the opening months of 1942. Except for Britain, Europe was prostrate; and German armies lay at the gates of Moscow. A revived Africa Corps under General Erwin Rommel was preparing to run wild in North Africa, and convoy losses in 1941 were 1,299 ships. In the Pacific, it was even worse. The Japanese occupied many Pacific Islands, Hong Kong, Singapore, the Philippines, Formosa (Taiwan), southern Burma, Manchuria, French Indochina, the Dutch East Indies and much of China. Only the Hawaiian Islands stood between the enemy and the west coast.

The war was coming closer to Canadians. German submarines were enjoying a "happy time" along the East Coast, while their Japanese counterparts prowled off BC. Several shore installations were shelled by these large airplane-carrying subs including Estevan Point lighthouse on Vancouver Island's west coast—the only place in Canada to come under enemy shellfire during the Second World War. To underline the threat Japanese raiders released hundreds of phony periscopes—a bamboo pole weighted at one end to stand upright in the water. One of these dummies led to a much trumpeted "sinking" off Gordon Head near Victoria, BC. In fact there were only nine Japanese submarines off the West Coast in

December 1941, and most were soon withdrawn to Hawaii to search for warships—a much more valuable quarry.

Not surprisingly, paranoia reigned supreme. To many it seemed a large-scale invasion of the sparsely populated areas of the West Coast was a certainty. Vancouver Island, Haida Gwaii and Alaska seemed the most vulnerable. Jittery observers spotted imaginary Japanese aircraft over Vancouver, Victoria and Prince Rupert. Some claimed to see cryptic messages etched on mountainsides to aid in enemy bombing raids. Spies were mistakenly reported at every turn. Japanese immigrants (Nisei) who had lived for years on the coast were suddenly regarded as an advanced guard for the invasion. Tens of thousands lost property (which was never returned), and were deported as far east as Ontario. Residents near the coast were told to block out their windows with blankets, stockpile food and prepare an escape route to the Interior. Harbour defences were beefed up, and searchlights with big guns were installed in Stanley Park in Vancouver, and strategic locations like Albert Head, Mary Hill, Duntz Head, Gold Hill, Macaulay Point, Yorke Island and Prince Rupert. The Canadian Navy requisitioned several yachts for patrolling, and enlisted fifteen fish boats into a Royal Canadian Navy Fisherman's Reserve.

But these innovations would do little in the event of an actual Japanese invasion. In late February 1942, Ottawa bestirred itself, and announced the formation of a coastal military force for British Columbia based on the British Home Guard. The Pacific Coast Militia Rangers (PCMR) was organized as an "irregular" militia, but would be commanded by a regular trained military officer to keep the men eligible for prisoner of war status if captured; otherwise they could be shot as spies or guerrillas. Professional military leadership had other advantages as well. No one relished the thought of large groups of undisciplined armed men roaming the countryside in the anarchy following an invasion.

Uniforms were rudimentary to save money and keep things simple. A PCMR armband was issued to be worn on the left sleeve, followed later by a small metal badge bearing the Ranger's crest—a crossed axe and rifle behind a maple leaf, a totem pole, and the prominent Latin word *Vigilans*. This pin is now a valuable collectable on eBay as few survived for long after the war. To encourage as many as possible to join, there was no age or health limit. As long as the commanding officer found you fit and capable of "ranger work," you were in. Fresh-faced thirteen-year-old youngsters found themselves serving with grizzled veterans of the Boer War in South Africa (1899–1902).

There was also no regular pay unless the force was called into active service, and no restrictions on leaving the Rangers or changing place of residence. Local training sessions were provided with courses in map reading, weapons, demolition, unarmed combat, wilderness survival and anti-tank tactics. One Ranger described the manoeuvres, or "schemes" as they were called, as a "hell of a lot of fun in the woods." And there was always the possibility of "a bit of meat for the pot" thrown in for good measure. Word soon got out, and within a few months ten thousand had enlisted in 126 companies stretching from Victoria to Dawson City in the Yukon. By 1944 the numbers topped fifteen thousand. For those who were interested in learning more military skills, a training camp was organized by the Royal Canadian Engineers at Vedders Crossing near Sardis in the Fraser Valley. But only a tiny fraction of the men ever received instruction from professionals. Areas of military responsibility were based on game districts because these best followed the local terrain. Hunters and fishermen were especially valued for their intimate knowledge of an area. Each company was expected to develop its own "personality" and was encouraged to find its own niche in the bush.

At first, the men were told to bring their own arms from home, mostly shotguns and hunting rifles, which would have created a logistical nightmare for ammunition had an invasion actually materialized. To remedy this, a few old Lee Enfield 303s from the Great War were offered to those without, and the Canadian government later initiated a generous program where a recruit could purchase a Winchester Model 94 or Marlin 30-30 for five dollars. At the end of the war, the rifle would become the property of the volunteer.

In July 1942, a new and formidable weapon was added to the arsenal—every tenth to fifteenth man received a Mark 2 Sten submachine gun. Designed by two British engineers in 1941, the Sten provided a critical stopgap automatic weapon for that country's woefully unprepared military. It was a crude and ugly beast, but simple to operate, easy to hide and amazingly cheap to produce at about £1.5 Sterling each. The magazine jutted out an awkward ninety degrees from the barrel, and it held about thirty 9-mm cartridges. Set on automatic the Sten had a high rate of fire, 550 rpm, more than enough to fill the air with lead at close quarters. By the end of the war, hundreds of thousands were produced, including a surprising number in Canada.

Unfortunately, this new addition had a number of very nasty habits, which made it a mixed blessing. Metal burrs left in the rudimentary barrel sometimes caused a blockage and unexpected explosion. Hands had to be kept well away from the breech as the shells were ejected with such force that one could lose a finger. But worst of all, the weapon did not have a reliable safety catch. A sudden jar or careless drop of even three or four inches could set it off—emptying the clip in less than three seconds. Although no statistics are available today, this must have caused some serious mishaps, and perhaps even a few fatalities. Rangers were warned over and over to always carry their weapon disassembled and unloaded until the last possible moment. Several ex-members confirmed this view, describing how fun it was to shoot, but "you never knew when it would turn on you."

An official magazine, *The Ranger*, was published, full of handy instructions on such things as how to attack a tank with Molotov cocktails, how to fight house to house, wilderness survival skills and how to identify, disarm and interrogate prisoners. They should be treated "humanely" and "protected from acts of violence, from insults and from public curiosity." "General binding of prisoners of war is strictly forbidden" under the Geneva Convention of 1929. There were also respectful assessments of Japanese military capabilities, instructions on collecting wild foods and methods for telling Japanese infiltrators apart from friendly Asians. "The eye of the Japanese is set at a slant to the nose; his teeth tend to 'buck' or protrude; the nose lacks a distinct bridge. The eye of the Chinese is set like that of the European, but it has a marked squint."

As the war wound down and the Japanese were confined more and more to their home islands, the magazine's tone became ever more shrill. Ranger numbers were drastically cut in late 1943, and great ingenuity was needed to keep the men interested, and convinced they still had a role to play in the war. Take this loopy example from *The Ranger*, by an imaginary Japanese officer in 1944:

> I am a Jap Strategist. I am happy to see that the people [west coast] are gradually relaxing their vigilance—oh yes, I know—my agents keep me "well informed." My only wish is that I could be in British Columbia to watch the fun when my brilliant attack starts... I will send two submarines each carrying forty well-trained soldiers, to visit two small coastal towns in BC. The leaders of their raiding parties will know the towns well.
>
> As soon as they set fire to their respective towns and kill as many as possible, our 80 men will leave as suddenly as they came. They will go inland to set forest fires, derail trains, blow up bridges, and keep up their work until they are all killed. What confusion it will cause! The terrified civilian population will demand military protection. Thousands of United Nations soldiers will be called from active fronts to protect the new front... Our 80 men—a paltry drop in the bucket—will

in this way cause a delaying action that will give us valuable time to prolong the war and increase the war weariness that we count on to win the war for us... The thing that amuses me most of all is that so many people on the Pacific Coast think that such an idea as I am going to carry out is fantastic. It reads like a storybook to them...

Perhaps the Canadian authorities did too good a job in the propaganda department. One elderly Ranger I talked to remains convinced that large caches of Japanese supplies still lie hidden on remote islands of our north coast. The invasion was only stopped at the last possible moment, he believes. And according to him, some old soldiers even know where these ancient tools of war lie hidden, still covered in grease and cobwebs. Oh, if only that were so! Imagine the collector value today of a pristine squadron of Japanese Zero airplanes.

But eighty years after the end of hostilities it seems highly unlikely that any such stockpiles will ever be uncovered in British Columbia. Even the widely held belief that enemy spy rings were operating on the West Coast prior to and during the war has been proven a myth. Not one Japanese was ever put on trial for espionage in the US or Canada. But the ironies do not end here. Intelligence information intercepted by the US "Magic" code-breakers, and released after the war's end, show that some Americans knew all along that British Columbia was never a target for invasion.

The US had a long history of breaking Japanese ciphers. It began in 1923 when a US Naval officer obtained a stolen copy of a codebook used by the Japanese during World War I. In 1930 the Japanese changed their system making it ever more complex—but they continued to send some messages in the old code. Not surprisingly within a few months this new encryption scheme had been cracked as well. In 1940, the Japanese inaugurated their last and most complex system, which was based in a modified Enigma machine. Within a year it too had fallen prey to the US Army Signals Intelligence Service (SIS).

By early 1942, these code-breakers had determined conclusively that Attu, Kiska and Dutch Harbor in Alaska's Aleutian Archipelago, along with the island of Midway, would be the next targets for the Japanese—not British Columbia. When the US insisted that the bulk of war material should go to Alaska in the spring, the Canadian government proved reluctant, and some officers openly complained. Sending supplies to Alaska left a big hole in the defence of Vancouver Island. But what could the Americans do? The breaking of these Japanese ciphers was one of the greatest victories of the war. It proved of vital importance in every major engagement from 1941–45, yet its effectiveness depended on absolute and complete secrecy. Access to Magic was even denied to many highly placed military planners in Washington, which led to much bad feeling at the war's end. In June 1942, the Americans were proven dead on about the enemy's intentions—the Japanese launched a combined attack on Midway Island and the Aleutians.

Pacific Coast Militia Rangers had the misfortune (or luck) to be forever chasing shadows, but their role in the war should not be underestimated. The Rangers provided a rallying spirit of hope in the early years of the war when people felt helpless and vulnerable. And after the fall of Attu and Kiska in the Aleutians, they gave us much-needed eyes and ears along the remote parts of the West Coast, allowing all Canadians to sleep a little easier.

Further Reading for the 1939-45 War on our West Coast:

Coyle, Brendan, *War On Our Doorstep*. Surrey, BC: Heritage House Publishing Ltd., 2002.

Webber, Bert, *The Silent Siege III*. Medford, OR: Webb Research Group, 1992.

THE GREAT POX

Evicting the First Nations from Victoria made a bad situation much worse. It spread the seeds of smallpox far and wide as infected victims made their way home. The colonial government in Victoria understood perfectly well what the results would be. They argued it was God's will. In many ways it rivalled the terrible treatment later afforded the Indigenous children caught up in the residential school system, but in this case the fatalities were much greater as thousands died.

On March 22, 1862, an inconspicuous notice appeared in the Victoria *British Colonist*. A resident of New Westminster, recently returned from San Francisco by steamer, had come down with variola, or smallpox. Fortunately, the paper reported, "the case is not considered serious." These words were to herald in the worst recorded disaster ever to strike British Columbia. By the time it was over, the smallpox epidemic of 1862 had claimed the lives of one-third of BC's Indigenous Peoples—at least twenty thousand of an estimated population of sixty thousand—and a few dozen white people as well.

Before the arrival of the European settler, the population density of Indigenous Peoples on the West Coast was greater than anywhere else on the continent. Most of them lived in what is today BC, where a benign climate and abundant local food supported large populations. We do not know exactly how many people lived on the BC coast before the first censuses were organized in the 1880s. Newspapers of the 1860s often quoted a pre-conquest figure of thirty-five thousand, but over the years we have learned the population was at least a hundred thousand. White settlers underestimated the size of the First Nations population, possibly because it was easier, morally and legally, to take land from a few disparate people than from a large, recognized population. In any case, official Canadian census figures show that by 1885, only twenty-eight thousand Indigenous Peoples were living in BC. A deadly combination of previously unknown diseases, alcohol, and firearms devastated the population during the first century after contact, and the numbers did not begin to rebound until the 1920s.

Of all of the white man's terrible diseases, smallpox was the most destructive. No written records were kept by traders, miners or the First

Nations, so the full extent of the catastrophe will never be known. But we do know that the smallpox epidemic was a watershed in British Columbia history. The sudden ravages of the disease effectively subdued the people of the First Nations and opened the door wide for conquest and settlement. The province of British Columbia would likely look very different today but for viruses, one of Earth's smallest and simplest life forms.

The little town of Fort Victoria was experiencing some growing pains in the early 1860s. It had been founded as a Hudson's Bay Company (HBC) trading post in 1843, and in 1851 Vancouver Island had become a Crown colony with HBC Factor James Douglas serving as governor. The town was populated by pioneer European immigrants and the local Indigenous people, who greatly outnumbered them. Trade between the two groups had prospered since the Europeans had first arrived, and in the spring of 1850 they had signed nine treaties, the First Nations trading land for goods with the understanding that "our Village Sites and Enclosed Fields are to be kept for our own use, for the use of our children, and for those who may follow after us…" One of these village sites became the Songhees Reserve in the heart of Fort Victoria. Indigenous Peoples, from many other groups travelled long distances to trade in Fort Victoria, and the gold rush of the late 1850s brought tens of thousands more white immigrants into town.

In a very short time Victoria grew to a bustling five thousand with a hastily erected commercial hub of houses, tents, stores and warehouses. By spring 1859 more than two thousand Indigenous people were encamped within 200 yards of the fort and several hundred more were visiting at the Songhees Reserve, including the warlike Haida from the Queen Charlottes (Haida Gwaii), Tsimshian from the northern mainland, and Kwakiutl from northern Vancouver Island. It was inevitable that whites and First Nations would begin to clash over conflicting social values and over competition for parcels of land. And, with a growing concentration of people and hundreds of ships putting into the port each year, it was also inevitable that smallpox, the great world traveller, would eventually make an appearance at Fort Victoria.

Toward the end of March 1862, rumours of the dread epidemic among the First Nations began to surface. Amor De Cosmos, the eccentric, flamboyant editor of the *British Colonist*, was one of the first to realize that the crowded town could be a perfect springboard for the "loathsome disease" among the neighbouring Indigenous population. He noted the unusual "susceptibility to contagion of Indians" and called for the establishment of a smallpox hospital. Already the disease was rumoured to have taken hold in the Songhees Reserve, and Dr. J.S. Helmcken, the

Drawing of the Hudson's Bay Company's fort at Victoria. Image credit: Alamy HK4GN4

HBC physician, had been ordered to vaccinate thirty Indigenous people.

It had long been known that among populations never exposed to smallpox, the mortality rate was high, sometimes over 90 percent. When variola arrived in the New World with the early explorers in the early 1500s, the devastation it caused shocked and horrified even the hardened conquistadors. Early outbreaks in Mexico, Peru, Spanish Hispaniola, Cuba and Puerto Rico destroyed 50 to 90 percent of the Indigenous inhabitants. Hernando Cortez's victorious march to the Aztec capital Tenochtitlan in 1520 was preceded and made possible by a crushing epidemic that eventually killed as many as half of Mexico's thirty million people. In his book *Of Plymouth Plantation 1620–1647*, William Bradford described the suffering of the Pequots in Connecticut: "For usually they that have this disease have them in abundance, and for want of bedding and linen and other helps they fall into a lamentable condition as they lie on their hard mats, the pox breaking and mattering and running one into the other, their skin cleaving by reason thereof to the mats they lie on. When they turn them, a whole side will flay off at once as it were, and they will be all of a gore blood, most fearful to behold. And then being very sore, what with cold and other distempers, they die like rotten sheep."

Bradford did not exaggerate. Smallpox was one of the most feared diseases in the world, with good reason. At the onset, the victim developed a fever, splitting headache and knifing pain in the back. A cough and runny nose developed. At this time the disease was difficult to diagnose because the symptoms were like those of many minor diseases, but those first days were the period of greatest contagion. Anything touched by the patient or his bodily fluids received a deadly dusting of viral particles. A single infected human lung cell could produce ten to one hundred thousand seeds of death. On the second day the fever rose to 104°F. A terrible restlessness and sense of foreboding engulfed the victim, who was very sick indeed. If he was lucky, he slipped into a coma. Children often went into convulsions. On the third day a reprieve seemed to have been granted. The fever dropped and the patient felt a lot better—if he didn't know what he had. A mild rash began to show on his face. At this time the virus attacked the epithelial layers of the skin as well as the spleen, liver and other internal organs. On the fourth day the fever returned, and the victim's throat became terribly sore and his voice hoarse. The light pimply rash suddenly turned into hideous pus-filled pox wounds covering large areas of his face and neck. Thick scabs formed as if the victim had been badly burned, and in fatal cases there was extensive bleeding under the scabs which turned him black. The sores spread until they covered his legs, forearms and especially his back. As his face became swollen and distorted beyond recognition, the victim emitted a powerful stench. Severe sores in his mouth and throat made eating and talking impossible. Many victims in the last stages of the disease instinctively immersed themselves in water to quench the invisible fire. After the seventh day, the person began to die. If he survived for two weeks, permanent immunity was assured. After a month or so, the scabs fell away and the sores began to heal, but the resulting scars would disfigure the entire body, especially the face and neck. The survivor was seriously weakened by the virus and vulnerable to a host of other opportune ailments such as skin infections, pneumonia, influenza and measles. Smallpox often attacked the eyes and was once the leading cause of blindness in the world. It also predisposed the survivor to arthritis, sterility and heart problems.

It is no wonder that panic began to spread among Indigenous groups up and down the coast. At about the same time, reports surfaced that "vaccine scabs" were being sold among them. Scabs were carefully collected from smallpox victims, dried for several days or weeks and hawked for "two bits apiece." A scab was then bound into scarified skin on the arm of a healthy person. If the disease took, the arm became red and swollen and a low fever developed. With luck, the patient recovered in a few days and was immune to smallpox for life. No one knew why this kind of vaccination, or "variolation" as it was called, was effective (viruses were not even understood until 1907), but it had been used for centuries in Africa, India and China. In fact, the "advanced" countries of Europe were among the last to accept variolation.

The procedure was certainly not foolproof. Some 3 to 6 percent of those variolated, contracted the full-blown disease and died. There was the chance of accidentally spreading some other dangerous infection such as tuberculosis or syphilis. Also the smallpox virus remained extremely contagious, and new epidemics could easily be sparked off by those who had recently been variolated. They felt only a little under the weather, and went on travelling, trading and living pretty much as usual—scattering the deadly seeds of the virus everywhere they went. This was well understood at the time. At the height of the epidemic, the *Victoria Press* reported that one patient at the "Indian" hospital, a variolated woman, "will not keep to her room, but walks about and was even engaged in making bread for some 'tillicums' who if they do not come to grief after eating it, may certainly esteem themselves lucky." Informed observers knew that variolation had to be combined with some form of quarantine to keep the pox from spreading. Yet there is no evidence that anyone proposed large-scale variolation combined with quarantine as a preventative.

By the end of April, Dr. Helmcken had variolated five hundred Indigenous People in Victoria. But with a transient population of over twenty-five hundred and no effective quarantine, the effect was minimal and the pestilence continued unabated. It quickly reached Fort Simpson, Fort Rupert and Nanaimo by ship and canoe. Reverend A.C. Garrett wrote to the *Colonist* of "fearful ravages at the Chimsean village" near Victoria. "Twenty have died within the past few days; four died yesterday, and one body lies unburied on the beach having no friends and the others are afraid to touch it. Those buried are only covered with two or three inches of dirt and it is feared that the disease will spread. Great alarm exists at the village, and it is thought that nearly the whole tribe will be swept away."

Two days later, on April 28, De Cosmos published a long and scathing editorial on the developing crisis. He predicted that the "savage occupants" of the local reserve "will rot and die with the most revolting disease that ever affected the human race." Chances were, he warned, "the pestilence will spread among our white population, a fit judgement for their intolerable wickedness in allowing such a nest of filth and crime to accumulate within sight of their houses, and within the hearing of our church bells." De Cosmos declared that the Indigenous People should be evicted immediately, their village burned to ashes and their shallow graves thoroughly covered.

The Indigenous exodus from Victoria began in late April 1862. For many it was voluntary. The Songhees, sensing the danger, packed up suddenly and left their reserve. The Tsimshians were given twenty-four hours to leave their encampment and a British gunboat took up a position across from the camp to "expedite their departure." The Commissioner of Police, Mr. Pemberton, began to evict First Nations from Victoria. Roadblocks were erected, and the Tsimshian camp was "fired in the afternoon and every vestige destroyed." In the future such behaviour would constitute a war crime. ·

On May 8, De Cosmos again demanded total and immediate expulsion of the Indigenous people, pointing out that the disease had spread to all the different tribal groups near town—Haidas, Tsimshians, Kwakiutl, Songhees and Stickeens. He sneered at the $100 that Governor Douglas had personally donated for relief of the First Nations. "But what trifling it is with the lives of our own citizens to think private benevolence can afford the security for the public health that is demanded! or that it can prevent the Indians from rolling with the disease at our very doors."

But it was impossible to enforce evictions in unincorporated Victoria, where there were no health or sanitation authorities and few police constables. And complete expulsion presented economic problems. Fort Victoria would be paralyzed without the Indigenous people, who provided an indispensable labour force for the wheels of commerce. It was this labour force that probably received most of the variolations administered by Dr. Helmcken. But it was difficult to distinguish between the variolated and the non-variolated. And what about the Indigenous woman who had shared hearth and home with a white man for years and had borne his children? It was impossible to separate a mother from her children, and difficult to separate a man from his woman. Besides, if women and children were banished to the Indigenous camp, they could fall into a "state of moral corruption and turpitude... under the skillful education of the red-skinned friends of their maternal relatives."

"Only holy matrimony would make things right," argued the *Colonist*. Marriage would "make the best of a bad bargain and honest women of their paramours at the same time." And their children could live "free from the taint of illegitimacy." But the notion that marriage and "legitimacy" would protect against smallpox was only a cover for a deeply held prejudice against the mixing of races. Many of the settlers believed the "purity and goodness" of the white race would be diluted in the children of mixed marriages. "The breed remains," Dr. Helmcken said of the First Nations, "and will require a great deal of crossing to make a superior race." When the wholesale evictions at Fort Victoria soon proved unenforceable, and the colonial government issued special permits for Indigenous mistresses, many whites were horrified at what they saw as a moral cave-in. The best they could hope for was that the Indigenous population would eventually die out, or become assimilated into the white population. The vicious ravages of smallpox and other diseases could only bolster such hopes. Indeed, the death rate among them rose rapidly. Dozens of new cases appeared daily, and by May 10, over two hundred had died, a hundred on the reserve and a hundred on islands in the Canal de Haro (Haro Strait). The northern First Nations living on the reserve were given three days to leave, and when they ignored the order, "fire was resorted to for the purpose of compelling them to evacuate, which they prepared to do yesterday afternoon after their houses had been levelled to the ground." Whites were forbidden entry into the deserted reserve. Even at this advanced date there were no white people with the virus in town, and only one in the hospital.

After the last encampment had been deserted, some voices at last began to be heard criticizing the colonial government for inaction during the crisis. Two smallpox hospitals had been established, one for First Nations and the other for whites, but the former provided no real remedy to the Indigenous population. The *Colonist* reported, "Indeed, the hospital, so called, is only a place where the victims may die in a heap without being obnoxious to anyone, and not where they may obtain relief and attention as its name implies." The total number of variolations outside the white community remained pitifully small, probably less than six thousand in all of BC, and not all of these would have taken.

Another question arose: What had the "Indian" missionary societies done to stem the disaster? From the beginning of the British missionary movement in the late 18th century, trade, commerce and money had been emphasized as much as religion. The missionary societies were a valuable tool for Britain in capturing and taming the far-flung outposts of Empire. But the clergy was completely unprepared for the scourge of smallpox in BC. The chaos and turmoil of the epidemic, combined with mass evictions, undermined the entire missionary effort. With classrooms empty, almost all the money remained unspent. The local newspapers began to question the missions' inaction. "What were our philanthropists about," De Cosmos wrote, "that they were not up the coast ahead of the disease two months ago, engaged in vaccinating the poor wretches who have since fallen victims."

Meanwhile, the mass expulsions had the effect of spreading the virus everywhere along the coast. Smallpox was among the most stable of viruses, able to lie in a state of suspended animation for weeks, months, possibly even years without damage, and with an incubation period of eight to fourteen days it was perfectly adapted to wreak maximum havoc among a displaced refugee population. Almost all who opened their doors to the fugitives welcomed a killer. Mass infection was followed by panic and flight, which generated fresh outbreaks as far as hundreds of miles from the source. The villages, forts and islands between Victoria and Alaska became charnel houses.

Reports from ships' captains were published in the newspapers: "The ravages of small pox at Rupert has been frightful. The tribe native to that section was nearly exterminated. Forty out of sixty Hydahs [Haidas] who left Victoria for the North about one month ago, had died. The sick and dead with their canoes, blankets, guns, etc. were left along the coast. In one encampment, about twelve miles above Nanaimo, Capt. Osgood counted twelve dead Indians—the bodies festering in the noonday sun" (*Colonist*, June 21). "Capt. Whitford, while on his passage from Stickeen to this city, counted over 100 bodies of Indians who had died from the small pox between Kefeaux and Nanaimo. In some instances, attempts had been made by the survivors to burn the dead, by heaping brush over their remains and setting it on fire. It had partially failed in most instances, and fuel had burned out leaving the blackened, roasted bodies to rot, and pollute the air with overpowering exudations" (*Colonist*, July 7). "Lo! the poor Indian—Capt. Shaff, of the schooner *Nonpareil*, informed us that the Indians recently sent North from here are dying very fast. 80 or so pustules appear upon an occupant of one of the canoes, he is put ashore; a small piece of muslin, to serve as a tent is raised over him, a small allowance of bread, fish, and water doled out and he is left alone to die" (*Colonist*, June 14).

In Nanaimo, Anglican minister J.B. Good and the Vancouver Island Coal Mining and Land Company (VCML) worked together to variolate the Indigenous population in the town's reserve, many of whom were employed by the company. Plans were also made to remove the Indigenous People to a camp outside town limits on the Nanaimo River, ostensibly to lower the risk of disease for all, but as it happened, the VCML coveted the reserve land for a deep-water wharf. At New Westminster, the Catholic priest embarked on an intensive one-man variolation campaign. When he claimed to have variolated over a thousand people in one day, an indignant citizen wrote to the *British Columbian*: "The vaccination [variolation] of a thousand Indians in one day, and by one man, needs no analysis to expose its absurdity. I abhor alike that sectional jealousy which sees good only in its own, and that fervor which elevates men at the expense of truth."

The virus moved quickly up the Fraser, Nass and Skeena river systems. It spread from Bella Coola to devastate the Chilcotins, then it attacked the Southern Carriers along the West Road (Blackwater) and

Chilako Rivers in the fall of 1862. From the panic-stricken Carriers, it passed to the residents of Uncho, Tatuk, Cheslatta and Eutsk Lakes. "At first corpses were hurriedly buried in the fireplaces, where the ground was free of snow and frost. Then survivors contented themselves with throwing down trees on them; but soon the dead had to be left where they fell, and the natives still relate in their picturesque language that grouse used to do their wooing on the frozen breasts of human corpses."

Among the fishing camps of the Shuswap along the Fraser River, smallpox spread like wildfire during the August salmon run and then hitched a ride home with the participants. Prospectors from the North Thompson reported, "There are no Indians on the North River, as they nearly all died of smallpox this year." Whole communities were virtually annihilated by the disease, and some bands lost so many of their members, they joined other groups to survive.

Much farther to the north, William Duncan, that towering figure in British Columbia's missionary history, moved his flock of four hundred Tsimshians away from Fort Simpson to nearby Metlakatla in July 1862, to protect them from disease and keep them away from the evil influences of the trading post. The timing was perfect. Duncan variolated his charges and the isolation served as quarantine, with spectacular results. Only five of his followers died, while a hundred times that number perished at Fort Simpson. Events at Metlakatla serve as an example of what could have happened, had the colonial authorities combined forces and acted promptly and responsibly.

The short- and long-term effects of the smallpox epidemic on BC's Indigenous population cannot be overestimated. At least twenty thousand people were killed outright, and most of the rest were seriously weakened, some left blind and sterile. Whole villages were wiped out or abandoned. Elderly people were most vulnerable to the disease, so keepers of tradition, oral history, and complex skills like carving and canoe-making died in disproportionate numbers. The elaborate ranking system of crests and clans was severely disrupted. The deaths of so many title holders meant that younger, less experienced people suddenly became heirs to the names, crests, songs and dances of their lineages. When several bands united for survival, whole new cultural systems had to be worked out. Shamans and medicine men were completely discredited, paving the way for the goals of the missionaries. The social order in many groups was seriously eroded, just at a time when it was most needed.

There was a dramatic shift in the balance of power. Suddenly Indigenous Peoples found themselves strangers in their own land, marginalized by vaccinated newcomers who could better resist European diseases. Growing opportunities in mining, logging and fishing drew even more white immigrants into the province. By 1885, the Indigenous and white populations were about equal in size. "How have the mighty fallen!" De Cosmos wrote in the *Colonist*. "Four short years ago, numbering their braves by the thousands, they were the scourge and terror of the coast. Today, broken-spirited and effeminate, with scarce a corporal's guard of warriors remaining alive."

The smallpox epidemic also helped discourage the signing of any treaties between the First Nations and the new settlers for many years. After the fourteen treaties Douglas arranged in the early 1850s, there were no more between the Crown and BC's First Nations except for a minor one in the Peace River district in 1898. In fact, it left most of BC as unceded territory. The ravages of the disease only strengthened whites' assumption that the Indigenous Peoples were a doomed race—accounts of the time refer to the extinction of the "Natives" almost as if it had already occurred—and if the First Nations were all going to die out anyway, why bother signing treaties with them? The land was simply taken over by the Crown and passed on to white settlers. In the minds of many Europeans, the demographic disaster not only showed "God's anger" toward the heathen, it also provided vast lands for settlement, concrete evidence of God's good will toward the new Christian order.

There were complex reasons why white settlers in British Columbia were so unresponsive to the crisis, why whites were systematically variolated and quarantined while Indigenous people were driven off, sometimes at gunpoint, to die by the tens of thousands. In the new millennium it may be easy to pass judgement, but a hundred and fifty years ago the authorities faced serious obstacles when dealing with the smallpox catastrophe, much like some people's fearful reaction to today's Covid virus.

Both of their two best weapons, variolation and quarantine, were regarded with fear and loathing by the Indigenous People. Variolation killed a few of those who received it and often set off new outbreaks of smallpox. And because sores and skin rashes tend to look very similar, patients were accidentally variolated with syphilis, staphylococcus or tuberculosis. Variolation bore no resemblance to any Indigenous healing practice of the day. Pressing a filthy scab into one's clean open wound must have seemed a barbarous and blasphemous act to those unacquainted with the treatment. Understandably, many Indigenous people hid from the authorities, believing that variolation was a plot designed to spread the disease, not prevent it. Even when variolation was accepted, it was not effective without quarantine, which must have seemed a particular purgatory, to be avoided at all costs. For the whites who understood its purpose and value, quarantine worked very well. To the Indigenous people, a place like the smallpox hospital was a cruel prison filled with dead and dying people.

Another obstacle was the sheer speed and violence with which variola invaded a community. It struck without warning, and within two weeks virtually everyone in the village was either sick or dead. No prompt communication was available at that time, so it was impossible to coordinate an adequate defence. The chain of infection would burn itself out and move on, long before help could even be summoned.

But the strongest impediment to anyone wishing to stop the epidemic was the British colonial attitude toward public health. Today's view that promoting public health works for the common good was not a widespread belief in 19th-century England. Epidemics and plagues were seen as cleansing acts of God, both at home and abroad. For the powerful clergy, variolation and any inoculation were seen as direct interference with the plans of the Almighty. And "survival of the fittest" was not just a figure of speech. England was a class-driven society much preoccupied with the "problem" of its own rapidly growing poorer classes. Thomas Malthus's *Essays on the Principles of Population*, which starkly laid out the frightening effects of overpopulation, was published in 1826. In it, Malthus offered a coolly logical solution to the problem: "Instead of recommending cleanliness to the poor we should encourage contrary habits. In our towns we should make the street narrower, crowd more people into the houses, and court the return of the plague. In the country, we should build our villages near stagnant pools, and particularly encourage settlements in all marshy and unwholesome situations. But above all, we should reprobate specific remedies for ravaging diseases, and those benevolent, but much mistaken men, who have thought they were doing a service to mankind by projecting schemes for the total extirpation of particular disorders." Malthus's views were in tune with the widely held beliefs of the time. If the poor in one's own country were seen as a disposable burden, the Indigenous Peoples of conquered lands would be even more expendable. No wonder Britain was one of the very last "modern" countries to wholeheartedly accept either variolation or the cowpox vaccination.

Dr. Edward Jenner had published his groundbreaking *An Inquery into the Causes and Effects of the Variolae Vaccine* in London in 1798, presenting the first effective smallpox remedy that would almost never kill, and never spark off a new epidemic. Lymph from an infected bovine's running cowpox sore was rubbed into a person's cut skin and the mild disease, closely related to smallpox, gave immunity for about ten years. Cowpox could also be cultured using human subjects. Collecting and storing the infectious fluid was problematic in the mid 19th century. It was easy to make the mistake of collecting fluids from sores that had nothing to do with the pox, but that were still deadly. Mysterious outbreaks of other infections were quickly traced to the practice, and questions of safety were raised. Moreover, to be effective the viral serum had to be collected at just the right time during its ten-day cycle of infection. And vaccination had to be repeated carefully every decade.

Still, many English people rushed to try the new vaccination during a smallpox outbreak in London in 1821. And other countries were quick to realize its benefits. US President Thomas Jefferson vaccinated his own large household in 1801 and distributed the first cowpox vaccine to local Native Americans a year later, for whom vaccination was provided by an Act of Congress in 1832. King Carlos of Spain sent cowpox to his possessions in the New World in 1804, and Dr. Francisco Xavier de Balmis, the Johnny Appleseed of cowpox, stopped off at Puerto Rico, Cuba, Venezuela, Mexico, Peru and the Philippines, saving tens of thousands of lives. To keep the delicate virus alive, groups of indigent children were collected from local poorhouses in ports of call, and a few were inoculated every ten days during the long sea trip.

In Britain the story was quite different. Parliament passed laws making cowpox vaccination compulsory in 1841, 1853 and 1867, but no money was provided to enforce the acts until 1871, when dramatic events finally proved the value of inoculation beyond all doubt. During the grinding Franco-Prussian War in 1870–71, the inoculated German army lost only a handful of men to smallpox, while twenty-one thousand non-inoculated French soldiers died of the disease. A new smallpox pandemic sparked by the French outbreak spread throughout Europe during 1870–75, killing half a million people.

All of these factors, combined with the HBC's emphasis on profit and indifference to social welfare, would have discouraged any public health crusader in Fort Victoria in 1862. But the administrators of the colonies of Vancouver Island and British Columbia could and should have done much more to contain the smallpox outbreak.

For one thing, large-scale inoculation would have been possible. The safe and effective cowpox vaccine was available from San Francisco within three days by express steamer. It was widely known that the vaccine had been used successfully elsewhere—several letters were published in the local papers to that effect—yet apparently no public official or enterprising entrepreneur considered offering the vaccine, even to Victoria's well-to-do white residents.

Teaching people simple hygiene for smallpox would also have been a cost-effective means of slowing the pestilence. If bodies of victims and their personal effects had been immediately disposed of, lives could have been saved. If the sick had been forbidden to travel instead of being forcibly evicted, many more lives might have been saved. And some rudimentary form of quarantine could have been enforced.

Fears of a runaway epidemic in white Victoria were completely groundless: natural immunity, variolation and quarantine ensured that the virus would never gain a foothold. But instead of reassuring white residents and caring for Indigenous ones, the authorities allowed ignorance and yellow journalism to shift the public focus away from disease control and toward panicky self-preservation. Not only did the Indigenous victims of smallpox die in massive numbers, they also came to be blamed for causing the problem in the first place.

The terrible epidemic of 1862 was in fact the last of three smallpox epidemics that swept through the Northwest coast between 1770 and 1862. The first arrived several years before the European explorers. Captain Vancouver noticed the telltale scars during his first circumnavigation of Vancouver Island in 1792. One of the earliest traders in sea otter skins, Captain Nathanial Portlock, stopped by Prince William's Sound in 1786 and observed: "The captain expected to have seen a numerous tribe, and was quite surprised to find only three men and three women, the same number of girls, and two boys about 12 years old and two infants. The oldest of the men was very much marked with the smallpox, as was a girl who appeared to be about fourteen years old. The old man endeavoured to describe the excessive torments he endured whilst he was afflicted with the disorder which marked his face," and gave Captain Portlock to understand that it happened some years ago. He said "the distemper carried off great numbers of the inhabitants, and that himself had lost ten children by it... As none of the children under ten to twelve years of age were marked, there is great reason to suppose the disorder raged but little more than that number of years [ago]." In 1829, the American missionary Jonathan Green reported that about thirty years before, "the smallpox made great ravages" among the Haida. "This disease they call Tom Dyer, as some supposed from a sailor of the name who introduced it, though it is probable it came across the continent. Many of their old men recollect it, and they say, that it almost decimated the country."

The death toll of the first disaster is impossible to count, but calculating on the basis of other statistics in the New World, where Indigenous Peoples had no natural immunity, we can assume at least one-third of the people were killed. It is possible that the disease was brought by early undocumented visits from Europeans, but a more likely explanation lies to the south. In the 1770s a huge smallpox epidemic exploded throughout the western half of North America. The disease struck the Native Americans of the Missouri Basin and swept rapidly westward through the Dakotas, across the Rockies and up and down the Pacific coast. Annual migration patterns, and age-old trading routes for dentalium, abalone shell, slaves and other items, ensured that the virus was spread far and wide.

The second great pox epidemic to lay waste to the Northwest coast ran from 1835 to 1838. There are no documents on the event from BC, but farther north in Alaska, imperial Russia ruled the trade routes and careful records were kept. Smallpox was brought by the Tlingits to Sitka in November 1835. It spread like wildfire south to California, and north up the Principe Channel, to Norton Sound, the Aleutian Islands, Kodiak Island, the Alexander Archipelago, Fort Simpson and the Queen Charlotte Islands (Haida Gwaii). The HBC in the south made almost no attempt to variolate, but Russia made vigorous attempts to arrest the epidemic in 1835.

The autocratic tsars were among the first heads of state to endorse Jenner's revolutionary cowpox inoculation. Long before the vaccine became standard practice in England, Russia's Indigenous people were receiving it from St. Petersburg. Incredibly, the Russian Alaska Company's ship *Neva* brought the first cowpox inoculant to Sitka, Alaska, in 1808. During the 1835 epidemic more than four thousand inhabitants were vaccinated, most of them Russians, Creoles and Aleut hunters. But the rest of the Indigenous population was widely dispersed, and most regarded the practice of cowpox vaccination with horror. Problems with shipping and storing the vaccine also reduced the effectiveness of the Russian program. In the end, of an estimated thirty thousand Inuit, Haidas, Tlingits and Tsimshians, about ten thousand died, mostly because of their fears, technical problems with the vaccine, and communication shortcomings. Interestingly, the mortality rate in Alaska was about the same as that of the 1862 epidemic in BC, one-third of the total Indigenous population.

So, if each of these three smallpox epidemics immediately killed off a third of the Indigenous population between California and Alaska, and if further tolls were taken by the fact that many survivors were rendered blind and sterile, and if other imported diseases such as whooping cough, measles, diphtheria, tuberculosis and syphilis killed even more Indigenous People, the accumulated death toll is staggering. The pre-conquest First Nations population of British Columbia may have been as much, or greater, than the hundred thousand figure often quoted by learned authorities.

The last case of smallpox in the wild appeared in 1977 in Somalia. Only two repositories now hold the living virus for "scientific study": one in Atlanta, Georgia, and the other in Moscow, Russia. Humankind has been patting itself on the back for almost decades over this remarkable feat of deliberate extinction. But all over the developing world, and particularly in Africa, shamans and medicine men still treasure and preserve pox dust (powdered scabs of smallpox victims) collected decades ago. Attempts by medical authorities to collect and destroy this almost magical powder have been to little avail. It was, after all, one of the few treatments used by early practitioners that actually worked. Is the monster just waiting for the right circumstances to strike again? If any of the pox dust were still infective, a whole new and terrible cycle could be sparked off—this time in a world that is completely unvaccinated.

Part 3

EXPEDITIONS

Destination Gwaii Haanas

This gruelling trip took almost three weeks of ferry rides, driving and a long small-boat trip, and we never did get to the World Heritage site of Ninstints. Still, this was by far the most memorable of our small-boat trips. There were luxurious first-growth trees on one side of the mountains and the other side blasted by logging, super fishing and mushroom gathering, fascinating chats with Haida Guardians and faint remains of disintegrating villages all combined in beautiful weather except for a 60-knot blow at the end, which kept us stranded for a few glorious days. This article was written thirty years ago and some things have changed since then. The number of people allowed in the park is restricted for half the year so it's best to apply for a permit early. Many guided kayak trips are offered but for those who prefer not to paddle, a small skiff with an outboard makes this beautiful place accessible.

‘‘South Moresby (Gwaii Haanas) is a Natonal Park Reserve and Haida Heritage Site. "Canada's Galapagos!" the advertisement proclaimed, "See Canada's newest park for 7 days with 30 other adventurers on our 23-metre yacht: only $1,999." Nowadays four days for almost $3,000. I lingered over the brochures and reread the articles in the *Washington Post* and *National Geographic*. Frankly, our prospects for visiting this last remnant of Canada's virgin west coast rainforest seemed, in a word, dismal.

The main problem was money. With a car, the cheapest round-trip BC Ferries ticket for two from Vancouver Island to Skidegate runs to more than $720. A luxury, guided cruise on top of that was simply out of the question. But for the fanatical small-boater, perhaps there was a way after all. Our 13-foot Gregor welded-aluminum skiff could be tied to the roof of a station wagon and still be a full half-inch under the ferry height limit of 6 feet 8 inches. With an outboard, this combination would theoretically allow us to go almost anywhere with no increase in travel costs. But there were other considerations.

Would it be possible to carry enough fuel, food and supplies 60 or more miles (120 round-trip) into an area that has no gas, supplies or facilities of any kind? In fact, the park does not even begin until you get to the

Tangil Peninsula—25 miles south of the nearest road on Gwaii Haanas. We might well founder under the weight of our supplies. Some sort of fuel drop would have to be arranged.

Another nagging question concerned safety. Would such a small open boat be up to the legendary rigours of such a windy place. The Haida had navigated these waters for ten thousand years in graceful canoes using only paddle power. Even today they offer tours of Gwaii Haanas in the *LooTas*, a 50-foot Haida canoe. A brief glance at chart #3853 further allayed our fears. The east coast is largely protected from the ocean swell by a complicated series of channels and islands running from Moresby Camp all the way to Skincuttle Inlet, 50 miles to the south. In recent years this passage has drawn thousands of kayakers and innumerable package-tour groups. Surely, with prudence, we could survive.

The day's drive to Port Hardy and two long days on the ferries passed in a giddy whirl.

PREP WORK

Before we could leave Skidegate, a number of things had to be taken care of. We obtained the Fletcher Challenge *Forests For Our Future* brochure, which includes a detailed map of the logging roads leading from Alliford Bay to Moresby Camp. Available on the ferries and at tourist offices, this shows how to find your way through the labyrinth of logging roads. We also paid a visit to the Haida Gwaii Watchmen office in Skidegate and obtained the two $25 permits needed to visit the ancient Haida village sites at Cumshewa, Tanu, Skedans, Windy Bay and Anthony Island. The Haida people were helpful and encouraging. All had travelled extensively in the park and were happy to share information about topics such as drinking water (plenty), bears (few), paralytic shellfish poisoning (be concerned), good fishing and wildlife areas. They even made considerable but unsuccessful efforts to help arrange a gas drop. Indeed, fuel was fast becoming a major stumbling block because no one wanted to touch it without extorting big bucks. At last, good fortune and good advice led us to the government dock in Queen Charlotte City where we chanced upon the captain of the *Shu-Ling*, who was planning a trip into the park the next day.

A full five days after leaving home we launched into the quiet waters at Moresby Camp. It was hard to believe the park lay 20 miles away. Nothing could stop us now, we thought. Unfortunately, our skiff had other ideas. The 10 hp outboard that usually whisked us along was overwhelmed by the combined weight of two people, 17 gallons of fuel, camping gear and food. Our speed dropped from 15 to 5 knots. At just about this time several patches glued to the keel gave way, flooding the supplies in our bilge.

We puttered to a stop. This "vacation" was starting to look like a disaster. Yet just floating there was calming. The water was smooth, the sun was setting over the San Christobal mountains, birds and fish were feeding, the weather forecast was perfect. Bailing every fifteen minutes became the routine until later when I discovered spruce gum had a rejuvenating effect on split aluminum.

The shadows deepened as we chugged south. A 4-knot current in Louis Narrows slowed our progress to a crawl. In places, the narrow channel is only 60 feet wide but navigable at almost any tide. Follow the signs to stay off the gravel. We set up camp on Louise Island and rose early for the dash to meet our gas drop.

Narrow Dana Passage led into Dana Inlet, which cuts between the Tangil Peninsula and Talunkwan Island. According to locals, this exposed area around the Tangil Peninsula would be the roughest stretch of water we were likely to meet until Juan Perez Sound. No problem, it was sunny and flat, with a gentle northwest ocean swell. We rounded Porter Head and suddenly found ourselves in the park.

To be honest, it was a bit of an anticlimax. Much of the northern part of the park, such as the Tangil Peninsula, Richardson Island and Lyell Island, had obviously been logged. Large rock slides on the mountains suggested careless logging practices. Stupefied with fatigue, we arrived at Shuttle Island and our gas drop.

Over the next ten days we unpacked and camped on several rocky islets in Juan Perez Sound. At first it was tempting to keep on pushing right on to Anthony Island, now a UNESCO United Nations World Cultural Heritage Site. This is the best preserved of the Haida villages and about twenty totem poles still stand there.

South of Shuttle Island, the forest is magnificent. Immense spruce and cedar are festooned with delicate hanging mosses. In some places the butts of these giants were 25 feet across. Hundreds of jewel-like islands are covered with massive timber right down to the waterline. Mosses of every variety lie in a thick carpet sometimes three feet deep. In places Moresby is only two or three miles wide and a stroll over to the Pacific side would be an interesting side trip. We frequently encountered traces of previous inhabitants: cedar trees with strips of bark removed for Haida robes and baskets, piles of slag from defunct mining projects, and abandoned homesteads. It was a mystical experience to watch the sun rise and set over this awesome wilderness, hearing no sound of boats, airplanes, cars or people. As days passed we occasionally met a large sailboat or saw a float plane, but of kayakers and other small boaters we saw nothing. There is a downside to this beautiful isolation. In the event of engine trouble, bad weather, shipwreck or worse, don't expect to be immediately rescued. As you would expect of any wilderness expedition, always include warm clothing, matches, a cooking pan, food and a plastic tarp. An EPIRB (Emergency Positioning Indicating Radio Beacon) would be a good idea.

The tide pools were brilliantly coloured and full of life. Each reef became a fantastic garden at low tide. A plethora of bat stars lay scattered about in reds, greens, blues and purples. There were scarlet anemones, large purple sea urchins, lethargic sea cucumbers, huge mussels, rock scallops, abalone, red rock crabs and topshells.

It wasn't long before we made the obvious connection between the splendid tide pools and the fact that a lot of what we were admiring was not only edible, but considered delicious in many parts of the world. The next day I took a ten-minute dip and collected enough food for three days. The water was cool but not frigid and I could have stayed longer. It was a bit like having a private sushi bar in your own backyard. Of course we had remembered to pack the wasabi, rice vinegar and soy sauce. A word of caution about paralytic shellfish poisoning in bivalve molluscs: Fisheries and Oceans Canada does not monitor the Charlottes for this problem and the area is officially closed to the harvesting of clams, oysters, mussels and other bivalves. We steered clear of all bivalves except for rock scallop, and in that case discarded the red viscera and ate only the thick adductor muscle. It was delicious.

During our stay in Juan Perez Sound we visited two of the Haida village sites—Tanu, and Windy Bay on Lyell Islands. The watchmen there were hospitable, especially when we showed them our permits. I found it flattering when they asked which sailboat we had come down on. They immediately invited us in for tea, salal shortcake, and fascinating conversation about the history of these ancient villages.

The area was abandoned in the 1860s after a devastating smallpox epidemic swept through the Islands. Everything was left behind to avoid contagion. Photographs taken at the turn of the century show the villages still standing surrounded by a forest of totem poles. Today little remains. Many poles have been carted away to museums for preservation. Most of those that remain have fallen and have been overwhelmed by rot and decay. The legendary longhouses are now just holes in the ground with a few moss-covered timbers. A century-old spruce forest covers the villages, further smothering them in vegetation. All is fragile and fading quickly.

The question of how these sites are to be protected has become part of the larger question of Haida land claims. The Haida feel their presence on South Moresby since the last ice age gives them solid claim to certain areas. Many Haida were arrested in the 1985 logging protests on Lyell

Island—protests that drew national attention and made the park possible. Whatever the outcome, it may become necessary to limit access to particularly sensitive areas—as has been done in some US parks. In the summer of 1991 some six hundred people visited Windy Bay, eight hundred Tanu, and an incredible three thousand visited Anthony Island.

On what was to be our final evening, I flipped on the little weather radio we carried and heard the Cumshewa weatherman intone, "Southeast gales rising to 45 knots, rain, cold, misery." Impossible, I thought. The weather hadn't changed in days. To be on the safe side I pulled the boat up on the shore before going to bed. At around midnight we awoke to the most dreadful wailing and howling. Torrents of rain lashed down and someone had to stay in the tent at all times to keep it from being blown away. The sudden speed and violence of this weather change had a sobering effect. That little radio suddenly started to get a lot more respect.

The storm took more than two days to blow itself out and the weather remained unsettled. By then we really wanted to start the long voyage home. All went well until we rounded Tangil and started down Dana Inlet. Strong northwest winds funnelling off Redtop Mountain kicked up a mean three-foot swell with breaking waves. Perversely, as we headed for the sanctuary of Dana Passage the wind lessened but the swell increased and it began to drizzle. The wild motion of the heavily laden skiff made it almost impossible to bail, and everything was too tightly packed to start pitching things overboard. Good grief, I thought, this is how people get killed. At the same time, my companion at the tiller lost heart and ran for shore going broadside to the swell. This was a serious mistake and we came within a hair of being dumped. Reluctantly, we turned back into it, reduced power and crawled forward. The five-mile stretch from Helmut Island to Dana Passage took two long hours. Then the sun came out. We stopped, dried off, had a welcome mug of tea, reapplied spruce gum, and continued uneventfully to Moresby Camp and the end of the first leg of our journey home.

CONCLUSION

There is much to be said about small motorboat travel in this magnificent park. It's cheap, it leaves you with options in scheduling and privacy that you would not have on a guided tour and it takes you speedily wherever you want to go in a pristine wilderness that has all but disappeared elsewhere. This type of travel is also abominably cramped, and more than a little dangerous at times. A good-quality boat and experience running it are essential. Also, remember, the park is damnably hard to get to.

I wouldn't have missed it for the world.

CRUISING THE LAND OF THE KWAKWA̲KA̲'WAKW IN A SMALL BOAT

My visit to the deserted villages of Mamalilikulla and Karlukwees was haunting. The area was full of broken shards of stone tools, chiselled rock and stunning pictographs. So many lives lived on this small plot of land over thousands of years. I had the same feeling standing before the Parthenon in Greece and Mayan ruins in the Yucutan.

There was a time not so long ago when the islands off the north end of Vancouver Island were inhabited by a powerful and numerous people. Though many traces of their culture remain, much of this interesting society has vanished due to introduced diseases and colonization. There is perhaps no better way to get a sense of this ancient culture than by travelling the area in a small boat. We selected the waterways between Knight Inlet, Minstrel Island and Johnstone Strait because of their spectacular wildlife, protected waterways, and fascinating historical sites. Our boat was a well-designed 13-foot aluminum skiff with a 10 hp outboard. We planned to ferry our supplies to base camps, unload, and then explore with an empty boat.

The charming village of Telegraph Cove offers a good point of departure. Humpback whales, minke whales and porpoises are common in Blackfish Sound between Hanson and Swanson islands, and we came upon a pod of killer whales at the entrance to Blackney Passage. Shutting down, I watched their approach—a marvel of synchronicity and power. At 20 yards, the novelty began to wear thin. A slight bump by one of the 25-foot behemoths and our tiny vessel would have been swamped in frigid water a mile from shore. After a bit of heavy breathing on both sides, they sounded and vanished.

Passing Compton Island in to Whitebeach Passage, we stowed and looked for a campsite. Forest reached down to the shoreline and moorage among these rocky islets was difficult. The southwest tip of Mound Island offered a protected sandy beach and long flat area of midden above the tide line.

A terraced village site was visible here as recently as the 1930s. Behind the abandoned village, a dense virgin forest of cedar, spruce and grand fir invited exploration. Underbrush was minimal because little sunlight reaches the ground through the thick forest canopy.

Powerful tidal currents flow among these islands from the nearby Pacific, flushing and enriching the area. Birds and fish were everywhere. Small but delicious kelp greenling and multicoloured rockfish lurked among the kelp beds. To anchor against the current, we simply grabbed onto a piece of kelp. For deeper fishing, we needed a heavy 12-ounce cod jig. Salmon, crab and herring were more abundant than farther south. Surprisingly, drinking water was scarce. Having received permission from the Mamalilikulla Band Office in Campbell River, which administers the area's First Nations communities, we set off to explore. Zooming toward Knight Inlet, we circled the chain of bushy green islets that surround Alder Island. Then we continued to the Indian Group, where we found excellent camping sites; large middens indicated they were once well populated.

For several days we camped at the ancient Kwakwaka'wakw stronghold of Karlukwees, which commands the juncture of Beware Passage, Clio Channel and Baronet Passage. The site lies along 150 yards of sunny beach on a steep 20-foot shell midden. Plum, blackberry and apple grow contentedly with thimbleberry, cinquefoil, cow parsnip, wild onion and salal. Most of the dozen remaining houses lie overgrown about 50 feet from the beach. At the turn of the century there were scores of carved figures and poles here. Photographs taken in the 1930s show a few massive human figures standing like giants among the houses. As late as 1974, a totem was still standing. Today, all have rotted away or gone to museums, thieves and vandals. In the early 19th century, the Indigenous population exceeded a thousand people, but the place has been empty since the 1960s. A lovely spring can be found behind the village. Bear scat was everywhere, and yachtsmen at the float in 1990 told of seeing a half-dozen bears sunbathing on the house roofs.

The Kwakwaka'wakw did not bury their dead but placed them in intricately carved wooden boxes. These boxes were often placed in trees. Decay and rot have consumed almost all of the funerary boxes, but a few can be seen in the area.

The condition of the graves was shocking. Bones were strewn about in grotesque positions. Over the years, burial boxes had been looted for souvenirs and holes had been gouged in the midden.

❂

A week's exploration had put a sizeable dent in our 24 litres of fuel, so we headed for the store at Minstrel Island, stopping off in Clio Channel to admire the brick-coloured pictographs. These include three mid-19th century steam vessels along with a whimsical horse and cart. Small seaplanes buzzed in and out of Minstrel Island, ferrying tourists to Rivers Inlet and other fishing resorts. As we pulled into the dock, a crowd sporting cowboy hats with corporate logos descended upon us. I listened patiently to their tales of 18-kg salmon and 41-kg halibut. They seemed unimpressed by my beautiful 1-kg greenling. That evening, we set our final base camp on a small flat outcropping near the head of Turnour Bay, Kalugwis (Turnour Island). A large stream of dark water ran behind it and a beautiful view in front made for the perfect campsite—or so we thought.

We sped off to Mamalilikulla at the First Nations reserve on Village Island. Mamalilikulla was the scene of the last big old-style potlatch held during Christmas week, 1921. A fortune in gas boats, sewing machines, gramophones, pool tables, blankets, flour and money was given away to hundreds of guests at a wedding celebration for Dan Cranmer. The authorities arrested the participants and demanded the Kwakiutl people renounce their "heathen" and "unCanadian" practices and surrender almost five hundred ceremonial masks, coppers (which were the copper-cladding from some of the early vessels to visit the coast), Hamatsa whistles, and other paraphernalia. The artifacts were sold to museums and the money—$1,747—returned to the Kwakwaka'wakw. The unrepentant men and women were jailed. Over the years, much of this priceless collection mysteriously disappeared or went to private collections. In 1980, the remnants were returned to museums at Alert Bay and Cape Mudge.

An eerie silence hangs over Mamalilikulla. From shore you can see a single totem standing unsteadily behind the beach. Among the abandoned houses and schoolhouse lie the remains of downed figures—men, animals and spirits, which turn to mush at the slightest touch. Two massive, carved foundation logs set on posts testify to the great longhouses that once housed many families. We returned to Turnour Bay to find our campsite ransacked. After initial fears of a two-legged intruder, we took stock and concluded the culprit was a black bear. Our losses: the eggs, almonds and the precious Oreos. The next morning, a large black bear walked slowly up the beach toward us, eyeing us speculatively and flipping over boulders while looking for shellfish. When he was 30 feet away, I bellowed a war cry that emerged as a squeak. We persuaded him to retreat to the beached skiff. Clambering aboard, the bruin turned his attention to the outboard and rocked it back and forth. Stunned, I half expected him to yank the starter cord and roar off. Was this some kind of candid beer commercial or what? Next time, we will confine our campsites to the smaller islets and avoid this problem.

It is possible to spend a lifetime exploring these emerald islands but we ran out of time. We were forced to cancel our plan to visit the Kwakiutl village near Heath Bay on Gilford Island and so were unable to search for the remains of a Chinese Buddhist community and temple that existed on Harbledown Island between 1890 and 1900.

That will wait until next year.

IN THE WAKE OF
CAPTAIN VANCOUVER

This story tells of our first journey up the Jervis Inlet. When we made the trip the inlet was almost completely deserted, but within a year or two it was cluttered with numerous fish farms. Fortunately most have since been removed because of infestations of sea lice and various diseases.

On June 12, 1792, Captain George Vancouver, his trusted lieutenant Peter Puget and a crew of about twenty departed Birch Bay near Point Roberts in two small boats. Their goal was to explore and map the territory to the north, and hopefully to discover the entrance to the legendary Northwest Passage. The larger mother ships, *Discovery* and its tender *Chatham*, were left behind in Birch Bay because it was felt that small boats were more manoeuvrable and less vulnerable to the vicissitudes of rocks and tides than the larger ships. This system of using small boats for exploration had proven itself in the months before, when Puget Sound and its environs were mapped by the expedition.

Captain Vancouver's famous yawl was one of the two boats used in this journey. In 1984, there was some talk of constructing a replica of this vessel for Expo, and several drawings were made, from contemporary paintings and similar boats in Howard Chapelle's *American Small Sailing Craft*. The money was never found for this project, but the plans tell us much of the character of this historic boat. A 23-footer, it was beamy, full bodied and stable. Propulsion was provided by eight rowing stations—or two rarely used sails—and the boat was probably self-steering under sail. Heavily constructed to conform to 18th-century British naval specifications, this boat must have been a backbreaker to row. The *Discovery*'s launch, which also made the journey, was slightly larger.

Unfortunately, Vancouver and Puget did not stumble upon the Northwest Passage on this or any other of their explorations, but they did make a number of important discoveries. The two small craft passed the mouth of the Fraser River without realizing it, entered Burrard Inlet, the site of present-day Vancouver, made a cursory inspection of Howe Sound, and continued along the mainland coast past Thormanby Island and the south end of Texada Island. On June 17, they reached the entrance to

Agamemnon Channel and paused. It appeared to the explorers that this passage might at last be what they were looking for: a water passage that would lead through the coastal mountains that hindered their progress.

There must have been considerable indecision in the boats about continuing the journey. After five eventful days, travel provisions were running short and the crew was fatigued. Vancouver and Puget decided to push the men to the utmost, convinced that the elusive Northwest Passage was theirs for the taking. In consequence, Jervis Inlet was explored from top to bottom in three hectic days of travel. During the month of June, light at these latitudes runs from 4:00 a.m. to 11:00 p.m., and the explorers made the most of it, rowing from dawn to dusk and sleeping in the open. Exhausted and frustrated, they returned unsuccessful to the big ships in Birch Bay, arriving just in time to meet the Spanish survey vessels *Sutil* and *Mexicana* on June 22.

When I suggested to my seagoing friends that it would be interesting to follow Captain Vancouver's route up Jervis Inlet in a small outboard-powered aluminum skiff, just about everyone wanted to sign on. Except for logging scars, this spectacular fjord remains thinly populated and looks much like it did two hundred years ago. The mountains jump precipitously to the sky, while the briny depths reach four hundred fathoms, among the deepest along the coast. Paradoxically, most visitors race as quickly as possible to the safe, comfortable and free float at Princess Louisa Marine Park. A glance at the chart will show why. There is only one truly protected anchorage to be found anywhere near the tortuous twists and turns of this inlet. Unfortunately, most of the charm of this staggeringly beautiful wilderness is missed in the mad dash for the security of Chatterbox Falls.

Travelling in a small boat gives greater flexibility. Small boats can be easily beached on a high tide. This allows for a leisurely exploration of the nooks, crannies, creeks and riverbeds usually missed by larger vessels. When one wishes to resume the journey, simply haul the boat down to the water's edge and away you go.

Another advantage of small boat adventure is cost. A 12-foot skiff with a 10 hp outboard costs a bit less to own, operate and insure than a 60-foot motor yacht or a 30-foot sailboat. Captain Vancouver too, obviously felt more comfortable using his small yawl and launch in these uncharted waters, rather than risking the precious sailing ships that had brought him from England. Our fuel expenses were minimal. During the twelve-day trip, we burned 14 gallons of gas and covered an unforgettable 140 miles.

Safety deserves careful consideration. The skiff was heavily loaded, particularly in the beginning, and good sea sense was essential. When the weather got rough we waited it out on shore, and incidentally saw a lot that we would have missed otherwise. Fortunately, our 10-knot speed meant we were never more than five minutes from shore in the inlet.

Things did not begin auspiciously. The first leg of the trip involved crossing Malaspina Strait to the mouth of Agamemnon Channel. As sometimes happens, it was a windy month on the coast. Our heavy load, combined with constant 20-knot northwest winds with 4-foot swells, made travel completely impossible. As the days slowly slipped by, we waited for the wind to come down and cursed ourselves for ever conceiving of such a vacation. These moderate to fresh winds would continue for many days, and without the kind help of a fishing couple, our camping trip would have been limited to the backyard: we loaded our gear aboard the cod boat *LCW*, put a tow line on the skiff, and made a very choppy passage to Irving's Landing, arriving in the dark.

It was silly to look for a campsite in the dark so we made camp on the dock. Half expecting to be rousted out at any moment, we quickly fell asleep and awoke completely refreshed at dawn. Desiring to escape the ties of civilization and with a long voyage ahead of us, we set off immediately. We had decided to spend as much time in the upper reaches of Jervis as possible. By noon, however, 15-knot winds up the inlet and a rapidly falling tide kicked up a nasty following sea, so we pulled into McMurray Bay, near the end of Prince of Wales Reach. The bottom is sandy with a small, sheltered hook of rock giving marginal protection at low tide. Mooring with some difficulty, bow first, we set off to explore.

McMurray Bay has a small icy stream, a lovely sandy beach, and large numbers of shellfish with oysters and cockles predominating. Millions of oyster spat less than an inch across covered the rocks, indicating warm summer water temperatures. An old road cut into the steep hills, bypassing a dilapidated shack and shed used during logging days. An August 4, 1972, *Vancouver Sun* lay on the table inside with a portrait of W.A.C. Bennett smiling benignly at his cabinet ministers. The chart shows a small lake about a mile from shore, but we were unable to find it. The logging road made for easy walking, and signs of bear, chipmunk and squirrel were everywhere.

Continuing on the next day, our attention was drawn to a large creek called the Brittain River. Going in for a closer look, we found the tide high and slowly puttered among the reeds, marvelling at the strange world where fresh and saltwater meet. At one time, Brittain River boasted one of the largest logging operations in the inlet but today there is only the caretaker and the logging debris. It would have been pleasant to tarry here to enjoy the exquisite pleasure of swimming alternatively in fresh and salt water, but the day was young and we were approaching some of the most spectacular scenery in all of British Columbia.

Princess Royal Reach stretches about 10 miles, with stunning snow-capped mountain peaks following one after another in train: Mt. Churchill, 6,480 feet; Mt. Spencer, 6,005 feet; Mt. Frederick William, 5,585 feet; Mt. Crerar, 6,060 feet; and the twin peaks of Mt. Pearkes, both about 7,000 feet. One cannot help but feel awe when viewing this rugged and forbidding terrain. Just opposite Deserted Bay we shut down and bobbed about, taking in the view. This was a mistake. Almost immediately our reveries were interrupted by an endless chain of good Samaritans coming to our assistance, convinced that a small boat adrift in the inlet must mean shipwreck. After three unappreciated rescue attempts and the friendly perusal of a Fisheries officer, we pulled into a little bay just beyond Patrick Point for relief. A dry boulder stream bed traced its way steeply up the hill behind, while the bay in front acted as a giant mirror reflecting the snowy mountains across the inlet. The distant sound of running water encouraged exploration so after lunch we gingerly made our way up the boulder moraine. Footing was tricky and the climb hard work, but we were amply rewarded when we came across a crystal clear mountain stream among the boulders. We followed it, and quickly came to the source of the sound: a small waterfall cascading into the large pool at the bottom. Words do not do justice to this beautiful and isolated spot. After frolicking, sunbathing, and wading the afternoon away, it was time to continue onward.

As evening approached we headed for Crabapple Creek to camp. The sunrises and sunsets are wonderful here, but care must be taken in selecting a camping site. Crabapple Creek is typical of many of the creek mouths along Queen's Reach. Cinquefoil, varied grasses, glasswort and goosetongue may create the impression that these areas are above the high tide line. Nothing could be further from the truth. Reduced salinity from the fresh creek water allows these and other plants to flourish well below the high tide.

Indeed, as one ascends Jervis Inlet, the water becomes noticeably less salty due to the large numbers of glacial creeks and rivers that fall from the heights. What is most striking, however, is the colour of the water. The deep blue of the lower reaches gives way to a dreamy milky green. Interestingly, the marine birds, fish and shellfish do not find this loss of salinity disturbing and in fact, tend to congregate around the creek mouths. A cod jig on a hand-line is a must.

Over the last hundred years, most of the forests in Jervis Inlet have been heavily logged at least once, and much of it has been gone over three or four times. Today there is little logging, but this should not be surprising when one views the devastation caused by earlier logging practices. Great scars disfigure the whole inlet and rusty logging debris litters the shoreline. Navigating near shore requires caution, and care should be taken to keep propellers, anchors, and lines clear. Locals tell intriguing stories of steam locomotives rusting in the bush and logging companies who buried their equipment at the end of a job rather than pay taxes and transportation on it. Alas, we had neglected to bring along a backhoe so I was unable to check these stories out. Much of the debris such as large tanks, 40-gallon drums, hot water heaters and pipe appeared quite serviceable.

Continuing along Queen's Reach, we passed the mouth of Princess Louisa Inlet. This represented a real blessing: the endless procession of large cabin cruisers and stately sailboats ended abruptly as virtually all headed into Princess Louisa Marine Park.

Passing Smanit Creek, one of the few areas presently being logged, we halted to admire the large waterfall 100 feet up Slane Creek. The tide was high, so we motored in almost to the falls, cut the engine, and floated backward in the mist of spray and the thunder of falling water. Slane Creek provided an excellent campsite and we spent several days there. A large flat area was bulldozed out in logging days way above the tide line. Young bushes provide shade and berries, but debris from logging is everywhere. Interesting plant and animal life abounded—we saw a moth whose markings perfectly mimicked a yellow jacket wasp, and dozens of tiny, brilliant orange mites covering some of the mosquitoes. But no-see-ums were the predominant pest and we were forced to vacate the tent after great clouds penetrated the mosquito netting in the early hours.

Several trails lead above the falls, but soon peter out into an impenetrable second-growth forest. The falls are beautiful from above—but be careful. One false step and it's over the side. An old shipwreck on the beach reminded us that the water that presently appeared so calm and flat was not always so. Mooring is tricky here, with a steep underwater slope and enough junk to guarantee a fouled anchor, so we pulled the skiff up on a high tide and slept easy.

We took advantage of our base camp in Smanit Creek, unloaded the boat and sped up to the very end of Jervis Inlet. It was here that Captain Vancouver was forced to admit defeat and turn the expedition around for a quick dash back to Birch Bay. Fortunately, an Indigenous settlement lay at the head of the inlet and the hungry Englishmen were able to procure some "most excellent fish" in exchange for scraps of iron. Vancouver estimated his distance here from the ships at 114 miles.

Fishing is still good off the Skwawka River and rumour has it that gold can be panned from several of the creeks nearby. The tide was high and we were able to ascend the 200-foot-wide river about a mile to its intersection with the Hunaechin River. The pale jade-green glacial water moves swiftly and its opaqueness makes it easy to get hung up on sunken trees and boulders. The river threads itself through a large marshy delta composed of low bush, sunken trees, mud and debris from previous flooding. We coasted along the edge of this marsh, noting crushed grass and chewed stumps indicating beaver, or so we thought. Later we learned that the mouth of the Skwawka was a grizzly bear drop-off point for "problem bears" from all over BC.

The end of the Inlet is a First Nations Reserve and permission should be asked of the caretaker before venturing far on land. Hours passed as we wended our way along the riverbank, watching the waterfowl and trying to get a glimpse of our "beaver." The tide appeared to be dropping so we headed back to the river mouth. Suddenly, we were aground. Shutting down the engine immediately, we slithered over a submerged tree and ground to a stop on the top of a large boulder. A freshening southeast wind blew us harder aground, while the rocky shore raced toward us on a falling tide. Rising to the occasion, I stood up and fell into water up to my eyeglasses. After a considerable bit of ineffectual floundering about it was possible to drag the skiff back toward open water. The rapid fall of the tide here was truly amazing and ten more minutes of fooling around would have left us high and dry in the rocky riverbed until the next tide. Thank goodness we were empty. The wind soon picked up to 20 knots, creating 2-foot swells spaced closely together, but we had no trouble skimming back to Slane Creek. Travel to a new campsite with our gear was impossible so I settled down for a little reading.

Heading down the opposite side of the inlet for our return voyage, we marvelled at the vast amount of water cascading down the steep cliffs. Southwest BC was unusually dry that summer yet here streams were everywhere, fuelled by the melting snows above. The careful observer close to shore will notice several brick-coloured pictographs a couple of miles before the Malibu Rapids. Captain Vancouver never entered Princess Louisa Inlet because the expedition arrived at the rapids at the beginning of a falling June tide. That swirling 9-knot turbulence suggested a "small creek" rather than another inlet to the explorers so it was not until 1862 that Princess Louisa revealed her charms to any European. In that year, Captain George Richards, in the steam sloops *Plumper* and *Hecate*, explored and mapped the area as part of a survey that included all of Vancouver Island and its environs. Captain Richards tried hard to remain consistent to the spirit of Vancouver's original selection of the name for this inlet. Many of the place names, such as Nelson Island, Culloden Point and the Britannia

Range, all relate back to the original Sir John Jervis and his illustrious career in the British Navy during the 18th century.

Sir George Richards was one of the great figures in 19th-century hydrography. After his detailed mapping around Vancouver Island, he returned to London to direct the British Hydrography Department. While not known as a poet, he was deeply impressed by Jervis Inlet and had this to say about it in his *Vancouver Island Pilot*, published in 1865:

> Neither in a commercial point of view, as a refuge for shipping, or as a means of communication with the interior of the country, does it appear likely ever to occupy any very prominent place, as it is hemmed in on all sides by mountains of the most rugged and stupendous character, rising from its almost perpendicular shores to five, six, and sometimes eight thousand feet. The hardy pine, which flourishes where no other tree can find soil to sustain life, holds but a feeble and uncertain tenure here; and it is not uncommon to see whole mountain sides denuded by the blasts of winter, or the still more certain destruction of the avalanche which accompanies the thaw of summer. Strikingly grand and magnificent, there is a solemnity in the silence and utter desolation which prevail here during the months of winter, not a native, nor a living creature to disturb the solitude and though in summer... the reverberating echo of a hundred cataracts disturb the silence, yet the desolation remains, and seems inseparable from a scene which nature never intended as the abode of man.

We entered a surprisingly pacific Malibu Rapids on a slack tide and quickly covered the 4 miles to Princess Louisa Marine Park. Clouds socked in the legendary snow-capped mountains, and large boats socked in the view of Chatterbox Falls by mooring directly in front of it instead of at the free float 100 feet away. While exploring the small park and admiring the falls, we were periodically inundated by hordes of happy young Christians from the Young Life Campaign Inc. located at Malibu Rapids. Struggling against the surging crowds we were able to stake out a lunch site in a designated picnic area. After the singing started it seemed like it was time to move on.

The coast from Malibu to Deserted Bay is very steep at first, levelling out at Potato Creek. The five or six creek mouths between are all worth visiting, though two are First Nations acreages so small there is no caretaker. Permission should be asked in Deserted Bay if you wish to camp.

Interestingly, Jervis Inlet was the scene of one of the first confrontations over logging between Indigenous people and the new settlers in BC. In December 1874, Moody Nelson and Company began logging operations on a 10-mile strip of land granted them by the provincial government. Unfortunately, the province had neglected to inform or compensate the local inhabitants. A very explosive situation developed when the Indigenous people confiscated the logger's food and equipment while ugly threats were exchanged. At first it appeared in Victoria that the uprising could blow up to "kindle a fire that shall blaze throughout the settlement only to be quenched with much blood." Victoria newspapers generally expressed sympathy for the natives, as did the young confederation government in Ottawa. The feds acted quickly by dispatching the gunboat HMS *Myrimidon* with a judge to cool things down. Judge Pemberton agreed that protection and compensation must be granted and the dispute was resolved peaceably. Soon after, in December 1876, the Joint Reserve Commission granted seven reserves to the Sechelt Band in Jervis Inlet.

The northern side of the inlet is very sunny here, and the beaches are littered with granite boulders and easily split slate. Slate from this area was greatly valued for arrowheads and scrapers and was widely traded among coastal Indigenous groups. Vancouver remarked in his journal that the slate implements of Jervis Inlet were the first he had seen on the West Coast. Others noticed this abundance and the Westminster Slate Company obtained several slate leases on the Deserted Bay Reserve in the 1880s and 1890s. Fantasies of a new slate roof danced through my head as we coasted slowly along 10 feet from shore. Just what we needed, a couple of tons of slate ballast.

We spent a lovely night on the beach in Deserted Bay, the largest First Nations community in the inlet. At one time Deserted Bay was a sizeable Indigenous community, which included a school for wayward boys. The chart shows an abandoned village south of Deserted River, but we saw no evidence of this from the water. One fellow told us that his father-in-law had lived there as a young man, probably sixty years earlier. Deserted Bay has lots of mosquitos, but the spectacular view down two different reaches makes it worth it. Fish, crabs and prawns are abundant.

Almost two weeks had flown by and it was time to think about returning home. The wind disagreed and we were forced to pull into the float at Stakawus Creek for shelter. With the kind permission of the landowner, we took a walk on the old logging roads that wind for miles back in the bush. It was interesting to get away from the coast, and logging roads are really the only safe and practical way to do so. Sign of deer and bear suggested that the animals agreed with us. With a change of tide, the wind died and it was time to continue. We gazed longingly at the logging roads leading off from Glacial Creek but only had time for a quick lunch stop. Maybe next year?

We made excellent time returning, covering the 35 miles to Green Bay in under three hours. This cozy little nook on Nelson Island provides complete protection and allows easy monitoring of Malaspina Strait. After a restless night, the endless 20-knot wind miraculously abated at dawn and we easily made the crossing of this fickle body of water. Once we completed the crossing, the wind returned and remained fresh-to-strong for the rest of the month.

SMALL BOAT NECESSITIES

Sometimes small is beautiful, especially aboard an open boat in our world-class cruising grounds. Your skiff can open a world of new possibilities.

There is a myth common today that only those blessed (or cursed) with a large, ocean-going yacht can explore British Columbia's isolated coast. In fact, with a little planning and experience, many remote and enchanting destinations are easily accessible by small boat. Travelling by skiff the visitor is right in the thick of things. Small-boat journeys mean camping on shore, usually on sites that have served as convenient stopping places for Indigenous boats over thousands of years. And there's no better way to get a feel for an area than by living in it for a few days.

Exploring with a small boat takes you to places your larger vessel should never venture: up rushing glacial rivers on a high tide, into rocky bays littered with huge ship-killing boulders, over sandbars on nasty swells and through shallow tidal rapids. Car-top to a new destination, launch, and away you go, often saving time and fuel. When the seas get too rough, the owner of a small boat pulls up on shore above the high tide line and relaxes. Forget about dragging anchors, lee shores, chafing lines and other heavy-weather paranoias that often keep larger yachts at home. If you want to dramatically increase your speed and range, carry main supplies to a central campsite, then unload and explore in the boat with a minimum of equipment.

There is much to be said in favour of kayaks, canoes and other self-powered boats, but creeping age has dampened my enthusiasm for tests of endurance and strength. There seems little point in arriving at a choice destination with barely enough energy to pitch camp and fall into the sack. Thus, most of my explorations have been with a partner in a 13-foot Gregor aluminum skiff, powered by a 10 hp outboard. Take care choosing your boat. Some aluminum skiffs are designed for placid inland lakes and are not suitable for the coast. A welded-aluminum boat that's beamy and has a slight V to its hull shape works best. Other lightweight and strong materials would also be acceptable. Just keep in mind that sometime, somewhere, on a dark and windy night, you will be dragging that boat a good distance over rough ground—portability can mean a lot. To cover as much territory as possible, small-boat skippers hitch a ride to a remote drop-off point with a tug, fish boat or larger pleasure boat. This frees the more adventurous of the need for a return leg of a two-way trip. Another way to extend your range is to arrange a gas/supply drop.

If you plan to camp in a First Nations community, ask permission first from the local band office. To find out which band controls which community, call any band office. But most of all, don't let the possible hazards outweigh the obvious advantages of small-boat travel on our beautiful BC coastline. Plan ahead, be prudent and patient, and you will have a wonderful vacation.

And remember, anyone can do this. You don't have to be rich, athletic or even well connected. Our stunning coasts and varied islands are open to all. Enough has been written about lightweight foods to fill many libraries. Simple staples such as noodles, rice, dried fruit, nuts, powdered milk, beans, crackers, fresh vegetables, cookies, and cheese work well. Always pack extra food in case bad weather delays your return.

Keep in mind that BC is one of the few places left in the world with a mind-boggling abundance of easily collected and succulent bounties from the seas. Bring condiments that complement this vast free seafood bar: lemons, butter, olive oil, garlic, herbs and spices and the three pillars of Japanese seafood cookery—soy sauce, powdered wasabi and mirin cooking wine. Euell Gibbons' *Stalking the Blue-Eyed Scallop* remains one of the best sources for original and interesting seafood recipes. Finfish should be cooked because of the slight danger of parasites.

Before eating shellfish, find out if the area is contaminated by paralytic shellfish poisoning (PSP) in mussels, clams and oysters. Fisheries and Oceans Canada monitors this danger in most areas and will tell you what is safe or not. It doesn't monitor north of Cape Caution and says it is illegal to harvest bivalve molluscs (including clams, oysters and mussels) in that area. Fishing is wonderful, particularly in remote areas. I use a short, stiff rod with a simple reel. Lures can include assorted Buzz Bombs, and a larger 20-ounce cod jig for bottom fishing in a strong current. If fishing by trolling, a depth planer works well with various lures, but it's best to ask what's most alluring where you're travelling. Bring a crab trap. The folding types are best, and a crab trap can easily be converted to a prawn trap with a bit of ingenuity and some old herring seine net.

Finding good drinking water can present serious problems. Many coastal streams dry up in summer or are contaminated by giardia parasites (that cause "beaver fever"). As with shellfish, local advice can be helpful. Always carry a 4-gallon water jug and be prepared to boil drinking water if necessary. Taking a hand-held VHF in a waterproof case can give you peace of mind. Program Ch–16, Ch–6 (tugboats), Ch–72a (fishboats) and the weather channels into its memory. Rocket flares that burst at high altitudes are better than the hand-held variety, and smoke flares are important in the daytime.

Do not forget the appropriate charts and tide tables Both will add immeasurably to your trip and help ensure it ends happily. Tidal rapids near civilization such as the Sechelt Rapids at Egmont are clearly identified in the *Tide and Current Tables* from Fisheries and Oceans. In remoter areas, patiently wait for slack water before dashing through. Treat these rapids with respect. Tides can change with frightening suddenness, and a roaring 13-knot current over a shallow, boulder-strewn bottom is an awesome and fearful sight.

Some outboards include charging coils for 12V DC batteries. Electricity gives light at night with a low-drain LED lamp, keeps the radio charged and happy, and reveals wondrous sights on the fish finder. For those without a charging system, consider the new generation of lightweight and almost unbreakable solar panels. Some are already built into lanterns, battery chargers and radios while others can be attached to rechargeable batteries.

Other useful items to stash in your waterproof kitbag might include lightweight camping gear, a folding hand saw, a hatchet, a grill, tinfoil for roasting, binoculars, a hand compass, a camera with zoom lens, plastic tarps, bags and buckets, snorkelling gear, a gas stove, candles, tape and glue for repairs, tools, a first aid kit, wildlife guides, and a good book or two to keep you sane during bad weather. The weather on the BC coast is unforgiving and often unpredictable. Avoid travelling when the swell exceeds 18 inches or wind speed increases above 15 knots, especially when fully loaded. Stick to protected waters as much as possible. Above all, never let time pressure you into taking unnecessary chances. As with any boat, large or small, grant yourself a generous time buffer so a few days holed up will not put you in a panic to return to work.

Gain sufficient experience before tackling a difficult journey. Try Jervis Inlet or Barkley Sound before a tour around Vancouver Island's Cape Scott or Gwaii Haanas Park in Haida Gwaii. Learn to anticipate weather changes by watching wind and clouds... and by listening to VHF weather radio. Be sure to carry emergency supplies on all excursions away from your main camp. These should include food, a pan, matches, plastic tarp, warm clothing, VHF radio and sleeping bag. Something as simple as a tiny piece of crud in the carburetor could leave you stranded miles from anywhere.

Watch out for bears. Bears love campers and know from long experience that people in boats mean food. Keep edibles in closed containers suspended in a bucket from a high tree branch. Do not store food in your tent or leave it unattended. Camping on smaller islets usually solves the problem.

Part 4

Lasqueti Characters of the 1970s

DEMON ALCOHOL

Alcohol is a highly curious drug. Its effects are both hilarious and horrifying. It seems to facilitate relaxation and communication but at the same time kills thousands every year. Booze is the most common gateway drug by far.

L ate one afternoon while preparing to leave an old-fashioned inter-island party, we were suddenly deafened by a blast of blood-curdling shrieks and roars from high above. Looking up, we could barely make out a slight figure flailing about at the top of a monstrous Douglas fir tree. What the *hell*? The quiet late-party glow suddenly shifted to panic. Was this fellow completely insane? Was it some kind of crazy stunt, or a final call for help? The guy was at least a hundred feet off the ground. One false step and he would have been killed. Looking around, we were relieved to see that no one seemed particularly perturbed. Everyone was going about his or her business as if nothing unusual was happening. One turned to me and commented, "Oh, don't worry. He'll never fall. That is just Luke being Luke. He'll pipe down in a few hours, you'll see. Just had a few too many scrotches."

One of the partygoers had that very afternoon introduced us to the infamous "scrotch." For the uninitiated, a scrotch consisted of one part of the BC Liquor Control Board's cheapest Scotch (for flavour) combined with three parts of home-distilled overproof screech, usually concocted from the summer excess of rotting yellow plums. A very nasty brew, to be sure. Anyway, we resumed our journey homeward, glad to be away from a disturbing spectacle.

It later turned out our fellow party friends were only partly right. Luke settled down after an hour or so, and made it back to terra firma without incident. But the story did not end there. Still in high spirits, he wandered back to the disintegrating party to make more mischief. First he refreshed his supply of scrotch, and then he started tossing people's hats and drums onto the fire, now a mass of coals. Next he turned his attentions to the remaining ladies, now terrified by this threatening apparition. They wisely barricaded themselves inside a nearby cabin. Luke upped the ante by banging on the door, his ruddy face in full flush. He then headed back to the bonfire where, mercifully, he finally collapsed into unconsciousness. It would be a long time before Luke was invited to another island party.

But the night was young. My dear friend and neighbour, Lucy, awoke to the strange sensation of something very large and naked moving under her bed clothes. Being fearless and resourceful, Lucy bounded out of bed and affixed her left hand to Luke's earlobe. She then escorted him across the floor and down a difficult spiral staircase as he begged for mercy.

"Please, I haven't any clothes."

"That's your tough luck," Lucy said as she sent him on a five-mile walk to his cabin.

So who was this death-defying maniac? I got a chance to talk to him a few weeks later. Neatly dressed with a clean-shaven face, Luke seemed like a regular kind of guy—polite, intelligent, restrained, affable, and helpful—even sweet. He claimed to despise drink and drunkenness. And, his one wish in life was to go back to school and become a criminologist—which seemed a little odd, as Luke seemed eager to involve himself in any and all manner of criminal activities. First, it was a vast pot plantation—right next to the biggest hippie-hater on the island. Then it was a fancy custom distillery producing world-class whisky and gin—then a pot smoker's tasting room/hotel modelled on the Amsterdam pot cafés. It all sounded feasible until Luke had a drink. Then, everything changed. He suddenly became an unpredictable wild man yelling and cursing his closest friends, sometimes ecstatically ripping off his clothes. As long as the bottle still bore a trace of alcohol, Luke would hang in close until the bitter end.

I remember picking him up hitchhiking by the lake one afternoon when he was three sheets to the wind. He grandly poured himself into the back seat, but remained silent when I asked where to let him off—an ominous sign. I was on my way to pick up three brand shiny new rototillers purchased by myself and neighbours, on a joint order. We had all worked hard on the purchase for weeks, and the combined value of the tillers exceeded $10,000. They had just arrived at False Bay, and I was selected to deliver them to their proud new owners. What could go wrong?

When we arrived in False Bay everything seemed in order. It was a calm sunny day, the tillers were being unloaded, and a small crowd was drinking beer and playing music on the dock. It was a festive kind of day, and everyone was happy to be in such a beautiful place. We all got caught up in the moment and danced for hours. Unfortunately, the bliss ended when it came time to leave. I headed up the dock toward my trusty van— loaded with rototillers—and discovered to my horror that it had vanished. Damn, I had left the keys in the ignition. Instantly, I knew that Luke was somehow involved. I panicked, fantasizing a violent end for the tillers and van. They were ten feet underwater in the lake. Maybe they had vanished as part of an elaborate hijacking scheme? Could he have driven them off the end of the dock without me noticing?

I started asking around, but no one had seen or heard of anything particularly amiss. Fortunately my story had a certain resonance, and several people volunteered to help search the roads for any clues. We drove ten miles to Luke's place and there was the van, in the middle of the road with the engine still idling. The tillers were in the back, untouched. When I met up with Luke the next day I asked him about the disappearance. He looked at me blankly. "I have no idea what you are talking about. I just hitched a ride home, and went to bed," he said.

I remember another night when Luke somehow finagled or stole a small reflux still—a tangle of copper hoses, stainless fittings and marbles. Somehow, he had gotten wind of a metal barrel of plum wine that had mostly turned to vinegar. With the help of a young couple, they had hefted the barrel, 100-pound propane tank and burner into a shack, and fired up the still. The whole thing should have blown up in a fiery burst of glory—taking everyone along with it. But miracles still happen, and everything worked splendidly. The problem was that there was just too much booze. When I arrived at 10:00 a.m. the next morning all three were in bed half-naked, dressed only in soiled long johns. The young couple was unconscious, and Luke was quietly babbling to himself in what sounded like Ukrainian. It was a harsh scene right out of Charles Dickens.

A few months after this incident, Luke left Lasqueti for good. Unfortunately, his alcoholism had gotten the better of him, and his health was failing. We heard later that he had passed away peacefully in Ontario from the flu, which was very bad that year.

SHOW AND TELL

Sometimes in order to combat isolation and boredom, residents of Lasqueti Island resorted to creative solutions.

In the early '70s life on the south end of Lasqueti was a study on seclusion. Getting "bushed" was a common malady, and sometimes a month could go by without seeing a stranger's face. Mail delivery petered out midway down island. There were only three working phones south of Gline Road, and Ian and Bev's lone blue pickup, dating from the late 1940s, was the sole motorized transport on the south end.

One sunny afternoon in early June, I received a message that my brother and his family were contemplating a visit to our rustic squatter's shack in Windy Bay. He always seemed short of time, and I felt flattered that the family would even consider such a visit. A simple phone call was all that was needed to clinch the deal—but it had to be made immediately—that very evening. Though I had hardly seen another soul for at least a month, it was time to set out on my trusty Raleigh bike on a quest for a working phone. I was lucky for about halfway up island (or maybe it was two-thirds) I found a house with an electric light burning in the window—a sure sign that someone was at home.

Mr. and Mrs. X had lived on the island for many years, arriving long before the bearded hippie influx. They were both in their fifties, overweight with greying hair, straight lifestyle, and a formidable reputation as a family that represented "the best of old Lasqueti." When I arrived they were both finishing up with dinner, and starting to get ready for a Legion party to be held that night near False Bay. When I querulously asked about using the phone they were enthusiastic. "Sure, go ahead, I'm sure your family would love to see your little beach shack, er… homestead." With that assent, Mrs. X retired to the bedroom to prepare for the Legion blowout.

Mr. X, drowsy from his heavy evening meal, tried to make polite conversation. He inquired vaguely about the weather, while pointing out that he and his wife rather liked the new longhairs living in the neighbourhood as they treated their animals well. As we chatted away my attention began to wander until I suddenly noticed that a mirror had been set up so that someone in the kitchen could see clearly what was happening in the bedroom. It was a perfect 45-degree angle, and everything was in focus as I watched Mrs. X trying on an assortment of coloured bras and frilly panties for the coming party. Her husband droned on, and I forced myself to look away. "I am not a voyeur… I am not a pervert," I intoned. Yet it was hard to tear myself away. That plump fifty-year-old body was surprisingly alluring to the bushed twenty-something I was in those far-off days. The surreal show continued on for almost twenty minutes. *How could she not know she was on display?* I thought. It had to be deliberate. But before I had a chance to decide, Mrs. X suddenly flounced back to the kitchen dressed to the nines, grandly announcing. "I'm ready. Let's go!" For some reason her husband did not feel the need to dress up for the occasion.

In the meantime I had completely forgotten about the phone call. They waited patently while I phoned, and nodded their heads approvingly as I described how to find our humble beach shack at the end of a two-mile trail. But for years afterward I wondered: *What had prompted that extraordinary display, or was it just a figment of my overactive imagination?*

Many years later, long after Mr. and Mrs. X had passed on or moved away (can't remember which), I had a curious conversation with an old friend, and his story shed some light on the matter. He too had stopped by one afternoon to make a phone call. The local party line was active, and the phone was busy for most of the afternoon. As the hours dragged on my young friend was delighted when Mrs. X asked him if he would care to have some reading material to pass the time. When he assented, she dropped a pile of magazines on his lap on the way out. After she left he peered down, and discovered the magazines were all 1960s style pornos with fanciful titles like *Spanky*, *Bondage Buddies* and *Little Pecker*. Unlike myself, my friend confessed that he was out the door and gone within seconds.

THE TRAGIC DEATH OF ROCK AND ROLL STEVE

At times all that's needed is a sense of humour to bring levity to a difficult situation.

Sometimes relationships just don't work out. When Jack and Jill moved into a dilapidated house on Lasqueti Island they thought they had found paradise. The couple had arrived in the *Artful Dodger*, a lovely old wooden sailboat; and they quickly became a part of the small hippie social circle on the island. After a few months, we heard the happy news that Jill was with child, and within the appointed time, young Ocean was delivered. All was happiness and light for the first few months until the new addition suddenly came down with a galloping case of the runs. Being an imaginative and creative sort of person, Jill immediately diagnosed the problem as cholera. For some reason the quirky diagnosis set off a round of discord in the relationship. Matters soon went from bad to worse, and Jack was summarily banished from the house.

A woman tending a sickly child by herself gets lonely surprisingly quickly. Fortunately, there was a large crop of poverty-stricken young men passing through that winter, and one of them could see that Jill needed a little comforting. Rock and Roll Steve was a handsome fellow in his early thirties. He spoke with a cultured Irish brogue and claimed to be a failed Jesuit priest who had fallen afoul of his oath of chastity. He was a natty dresser who would suddenly break out in high Latin liturgy during a lull in the conversation. The ex-priest also affected a strong musical fondness for the guitar, though the only tune we ever heard him play was "I am the Walrus" by the Beatles—over and over and over again. Unfortunately, Steve's other claim to fame was his feet, which exuded a mind-boggling aroma the instant he removed his gumboots.

At first it seemed Steve was solidly in Jill's good graces. But the repetitive music and smelly feet soon exacted a frightful toll. Within a couple of weeks, it was apparent that Jill had begun to tire of her new lover. Steve soon noticed the lack of interest and became tiresome. He valued the free food, a roof over his head, and the warm comfort of his bedmate. They quarrelled, and Steve threatened drastic action. He dramatically announced to the world that he would simply kill himself if she dumped him. Jill was not deterred and told him quite bluntly to decamp.

"All right, if that's what you really want," was all he said.

The next morning the couch was empty, and he had gone. But his wallet (with $75), sleeping bag, guitar and clothes remained. Jill was completely convinced that her ex-priest had followed up on this threat. "Oh God, I know he's out there somewhere, lying cold and dead in the savage bush, and all on account of me." The whole neighbourhood was soon in a stew about the apparent suicide, but had he really gone and done himself in?

Two schools of thought soon evolved. The romantics saw it as a Romeo and Juliet kind of thing. Jill had broken his heart, and he had taken the ultimate revenge. The money and other stuff he had left behind proved it. After all, there is no value in earthly possessions after death. But cynical sceptics pointed out that this was not the romance of the century, and that they had only been together two weeks. He could easily have caught a ride off island on one of the hundreds of small sports fishing boats that frequented the island in those salmon-rich times. Maybe it was more a case of crass mind games rather than a vengeful suicide.

For the next month we all kept our eyes open for suspicious activity among the vulture and eagle population. An old ram, one of the ownerless feral sheep, who passed away of natural causes in a nearby field, created a sudden flurry of excitement. I made several expeditions down to the shoreline looking for a suicide note, or perhaps a matching pair of gumboots. But there was nothing. Someone suggested that we notify air-sea rescue and report Steve as missing, but the phones were out, as usual, and anyway, no one knew his true name, or even that he was really missing. Then as now, Lasqueti drew hordes of visitors, many of whom only stayed for a week or so before continuing on their various quests. So, we never got in touch with air-sea rescue.

After several months without a sign, everyone began to lose interest. We took his dirty clothes and sleeping bag up to the Free Store and spent his money on several bottles of Bushmills Irish whiskey. After all, he had always demonstrated a pronounced fondness for high-class booze.

Suddenly, there was an unexpected break in the case. Late one night a neighbour was chatting over a beer in the Rod and Gun in Parksville. He had just ordered a second round when he noticed a faint but familiar aroma wafting through the bar. Then a song began to play on the jukebox, an old Beatles tune about walruses. Our friend looked up sharply and did a double take, for there was Rock and Roll Steve, in the flesh, sitting at the bar with a comely young lady. He coolly sipped a beer, drumming his fingers in time to the music, giving no overt sign of recognition. Then as the music ended, Steve tipped his hat to the bartender, flashed a quick wink to his ex-neighbour, and walked out with his pretty companion into the night.

POOR MAN'S ROCK REVISITED

The incredible abundance of salmon in the lower Salish Sea is evident in Bertrand Sinclair's 1920 novel, *Poor Man's Rock*. When I arrived in the mid-seventies, the fishing was still somewhat productive but by the time I wrote the article in 2012 it was almost non-existent. The combination of overfishing, salmon farming, encroaching civilization and global warming has been ruinous.

What was British Columbia's coastal environment like sixty years ago—eighty years ago—a hundred years ago? This is not an easy question. Photos were few, and most fail to capture the subtleties of a marine environment. Memories of "old-timers" become dim after a few decades, and rarely extend back beyond sixty years. Perhaps the most vivid windows to the past are the scribblings of diarists, poets, explorers, scientists, letter writers and novelists of the time. Making my annual pilgrimage to Macleod's bookshop in Vancouver, I had the good fortune to run across just such a time capsule, a much-worn copy of the novel *Poor Man's Rock* written in 1920 by Bertrand Sinclair. Although almost unknown today, Bertrand W. Sinclair was one of British Columbia's most successful writers. Born a Scotsman in 1881, he was an adventurer in the grand style, who worked as a cowboy, logger, and fisherman in both Canada and the US. Sinclair wrote prolifically, fifteen novels, dozens of novelettes, hundreds of short stories and poems. Six of his books were even made into silent films. He was strongly influenced by Jack London, and was a social critic who felt that monetary gain must not destroy beauty or create waste. Sinclair despised those who produce no wealth but made their living manipulating others, and was particularly sensitive to the wanton destruction of natural resources. He adopted the melodramatic style of America's Wild West action stories, but placed them in a Canadian context. The author settled in Pender Harbour in 1923 and remained there until his death in 1972.

Poor Man's Rock sold eighty thousand copies, and was one of Sinclair's most popular books. Set in Squitty Bay on Lasqueti Island, the storyline revolves around Jack MacRae, a Flying Corps hero from the First World War, and his struggle to become an independent salmon packer in lower Georgia Strait. Jack's return to civilian life was not easy and he had to overcome his father's death from Spanish Flu, bitter class rivalry, rock-bottom fish prices, and the domineering canneries that exploited the fisherman mercilessly. Salmon prices in those days might be two cents a pound for springs, three-quarters of a cent for humpbacks, and even less for dog salmon. White springs were commercially worthless. But relax, by the end of the book the hero has successfully beaten back the canneries, subdued his bitter rival and won the hand of the beautiful Betty Gower. But let's forget the predictable plot, and focus on the really striking thing about this book today. Bertrand's poetic descriptions of the incredible variety and abundance of life in the lower Salish Sea ninety years ago are sobering. Here are a few excerpts:

> But in good weather, in the season, the blueback and spring salmon swim in vast schools across the end of Squitty. They feed upon small fish, baby herring, tiny darting atoms of finny life that swarm in countless numbers. What these inch-long fishes feed upon no man knows, but they begin to show in the Gulf early in spring. The water is alive with them—minute, darting streaks of silver. The salmon follow these schools, pursuing, swallowing, eating to live. Shark and giant blackfish follow dogfish and seal... The salmon swarmed in millions on their way up to spawn in fresh-water streams.
>
> The cliffs north of Point Old [Point Young] and the area immediately surrounding the Rock are thickly strewn with kelp. In these brown patches of seaweed the tiny fish, the schools of baby herring, take refuge from their restless enemy, the swift and voracious salmon... The salmon run was long over, but the coastal waters still yielded a supply of edible fish. There were always a few spring salmon to be taken here and there. Ling, red and rock cod knew no seasons. Nor the ground fish, plaice, sole flounders, halibut. Already the advance guard of the great run of mature herring began to show.
>
> Poor Man's Rock had given many a man his chance. Nearly always salmon could be taken there by a rowboat. And because for many years old men, men with lean purses, men with a rowboat, a few dollars, and a hunger for independence, had camped in Squitty Cove and fished the Squitty headlands and seldom failed to take salmon around the Rock, the name had clung to that brown hummock of granite lifting out [of] the sea at half tide... Only a poor man trolled in a rowboat, tugging at the oars hour after hour without cabin shelter from wind, sun and rain...

As many as five thousand Coho salmon were harvested in a day's fishing off Lasqueti, and the abundance seemed unending. On those few occasions when the salmon were unavailable, there were other fish in excess of anyone's needs. Perhaps that is why the lower Gulf Islands were a good place to be during the dirty thirties a decade later. The Great Depression stole lives and livelihoods, but there was always something to eat even if one had to dine on seafood twenty times a week.

Needless to say, those days of plenty are long gone. None of the species mentioned can now support a living, and others like the halibut, black cod and basking shark have been completely driven from the southern Salish Sea. I have not heard of more than a handful of mature salmon being caught off Squitty Bay in recent years. Even the ubiquitous bull kelp that formed vast forests at the mouth of Squitty Bay and Poor Man's Rock have almost completely vanished, although there were still fragments in the early '80s.

A number of reasons have been suggested for this tragic decline. Reckless real estate development has wrecked habitat, and burdened the lower Salish Sea with pollution. Salinity of the waters has declined as the surrounding forest disappeared into the sawmills. But a major culprit must be overfishing. The prime money-makers like salmon are gone, replaced by the vacuuming up of lesser species—and everything else. How can the more desirable fish like salmon, snapper or halibut ever re-establish a toe-hold when their food and young are sieved from the seas several times annually? Look at the fishing regime around Lasqueti Island today. The shrimp trawl fishery in the spring tears up the sea bottom, encroaches on "protected no fishing areas," and kills large numbers of non-targeted species. Half of the catch or more is discarded as unmarketable—young rockfish, salmon, ling, water scorpions and crabs. Then there is the herring frenzy in February with the small meshed seine and gill nets. Again, nothing can escape these walls of death. The "incidental" by-catch is sold on the market, and it is one of the few times of year that fresh local salmon cam be found in area fish stores. And leave us not forget the mid-summer hake fishery. The area around Nanaimo swarms with boats while the French Creek Fish Plant hums briefly with activity. The seas are cleansed once again. We are creating a desert for the sake of a few jobs and big profits selling this rapidly disappearing seafood abroad. Removing this huge amount of biomass three or four times a year impacts everything else in the sea.

Bertrand Sinclair lived a long and productive life. After his passing at age ninety-one, his ashes were scattered off Poor Man's Rock. There can be no doubt that Sinclair would be shocked and appalled by the wholesale squandering of our marine resources today. In memory of one of British Columbia's most interesting authors here are two modest proposals. First, end—or at least curtail—all trawling and fishing for finfish in the lower Salish Sea for five years. The present no-fishing areas are too small and fragmented to be of much use. In many places like the south Pacific, large no-fishing sanctuaries have proven themselves to be economically and biologically viable. Within a few years, the fish caught in neighbouring areas are bigger, healthier and more abundant. Flushed by the Fraser River and Juan de Fuca Strait, the lower Salish Sea is immensely fertile and could become a highly productive nursery area once again. Second, spend some serious money to rebuild habitats destroyed by development. Billions of our taxpayer dollars have been lavished on grandiose and questionable projects such as military muscle in the Arctic, the 2010 Olympics and huge dam projects. Let's re-allocate a tiny fraction of that sum doing something more tangible—like restoring local streams and the Fraser River watershed. But funds for hatcheries, stream cleanup and restoration are disappearing. Even the tiny Lasqueti Streamkeepers Society was forced to stop work for lack of funds over the past year. Yet if we are really interested in selling Canada's image abroad, what could be more powerful than demonstrating the respect we have for one of our own most remarkable and renowned resources—the Pacific salmon? Our legendary fish have been feeding the world for over 130 years. Bertrand Sinclair's book reminds us again of what once was, and what could be again.

For those interested, *Poor Man's Rock* is available as a free download on the internet at *www.gutenberg.org*.

THE HISTORY OF XWE'ETAY/ LASQUETI ISLAND

AS SEEN THROUGH THE ARCHAEOLOGICAL RECORD

By Dana Lepofsky

The archaeological record can tell a different kind of history than what is contained within written and oral records. For instance, while the spoken and written words can highlight specific events, the archaeological record often tells the story of an amalgamation of events—all woven together in a single layer. That is, because of various processes that work on archaeological remains after they are deposited in the ground, it is often impossible to know if a single layer was deposited in a moment or over several years. Furthermore, the record will tend to be biased toward those activities that leave lasting remains, such as those involving stone tools, the construction of buildings, or the gatherings of large numbers of people. Evidence for remains that are left from many mundane, daily tasks can be much harder to find in the archaeological record.

The telling of history via the archaeological record is further complicated by the same issues as the written word: the telling is influenced by the teller. For instance, in the early days of archaeology in North America, the settler archaeologists saw in the record the remains of a Lost Tribe. They could not see the impressive Indigenous societies that had developed over the millennia. Such societies often involved complex systems of resource management embedded in intricate governance systems. But the evidence for such systems was ignored or not seen because of preconceived ideas of how histories unfolded before Europeans settled in North America.

The recounting of the history of Xwe'etay/Lasqueti Island exemplifies how different views on history can develop. Located smack dab in the middle of the Salish Sea of British Columbia, the island had a reputation of being in the middle of nowhere since it is separated by ocean from the major urban centers of Vancouver to the east and Victoria to the west. Beginning in the late 1800s and continuing to today, European settlers moved to the island because of its many possibilities: resource extraction (lumber and fish), agriculture, and the ability to be somewhat removed by the trappings of mainstream society. Importantly, the settlers arrived to a landscape that had no Indigenous occupants, only the occasional visitor to fish or harvest clams. The land was seen as *terra nullius*, and thus free for the taking and the creating of histories on a blank page.

When I arrived at Xwe'etay/Lasqueti in 1989, I was regaled with stories about the (lack of) Indigenous history on the island. I was told there never was a significant Indigenous presence, that First Nations stories said the island was not inhabitable, that the island did not have the food and water supply to support a large population, and so on. Even the name of the island—Lasqueti, supposedly named after some minor Spanish naval officer who never stepped on the island—reinforced this truncated view of the island's history. For some, this truth was supported by the fact that no descendant community members live on the island today.

From my vantage point as an archaeologist, however, none of this made any sense. Even on my first arrival to the island, I was struck by the extent of archaeological sites—some of which were among the most impressive I've seen in the Salish Sea. Even the island's Indigenous name spoke loudly to its central place in First Nations' history. Xwe'etay (pronounced *hua-ya-tay*), meaning yew tree, is the name shared by all Coast Salish groups who have a name for the island, reflecting its widespread importance. The name comes from an oral tradition that recounts the island's origins as a yew tree—long before the arrival of the Spanish to these waters in the late 1700s.

Some thirty years after I saw my first archaeological site on Xwe'etay, we understand that my initial impressions of the Indigenous history of the island were correct: the archaeological record tells of a long and intricate relationship of Indigenous Peoples—and lots of people—on Xwe'etay. We know about this once-hidden history through my own observations and by those of other islanders who now have "archaeology eyes" when exploring the landscape. As a result, over the decades, there has been increasing recognition that the ideas of Xwe'etay being "in the middle of nowhere" and being "*terra nullius*" couldn't be further from the truth.

Details on the Indigenous history of the Island have most recently been fleshed out in the context of the Xwe'etay/Lasqueti Archaeology Project (XLAP; https://www.sfu.ca/rem/lasqueti.html.html), co-led by myself and community planner Dr. Sean Markey. The main goal of the project is to increase awareness of the Indigenous heritage on Xwe'etay and to better honour and protect that history as well as its connection to Indigenous people today. Five of the fourteen First Nations with historical connections to the island are partners in this project and we are learning together how to accomplish this goal.

An important element of the project is the active education of both the settler and neighbouring First Nations through community events that highlight the extensive archaeological record of the island. We meet on the island to look at archaeological sites and to share food and stories, we hold information sessions at local events, we travel to our neighbouring partners' homes to share stories and project results, and we invite locals to participate in the project's explorations. Some of our First Nations partners and friends have held deeply meaningful ritual events on the island to honour the island's ancestral peoples. Over the years, there has been a huge shift in most people's thinking to now fully recognizing the breadth and depth of Indigenous history on Xwe'etay.

So, what does the archaeological record tell us about the Indigenous history of Xwe'etay? In short: a lot. Our surveys of the coastline, radiocarbon dating, and conversations with locals about belongings (artifacts) found while gardening, indicate the island supported an extensive Indigenous population in the past. People began settling on the island over seven thousand years ago—when sea levels were beginning to stabilize after the ice age. At first, people settled throughout the island's coast, but over time, they focused on the bays that were most inhabitable (in terms of wind protection) and were most accessible via boat and overland travel. Isolated locations, which would have meant people would have been far from social happenings, were not inhabited or only inhabited later in time. By a thousand years ago, much of the island was settled.

Archaeological sites are many and varied. We find evidence of large permanent settlements where the occupants have transported baskets of shell construction fill to create terraced living surfaces on which they built their houses. There are also several small shorter-term camps, many of which are located along trails between the larger settlements. We also find lookouts where people could have watched for friends and foes. The areas away from the coastline have evidence of occupation and use in the form of small sites or isolated artifacts that are the remnants of activities such as hunting and processing of deer or the gathering of berries for food or Douglas fir bark for fuel.

Our survey of the forests and the intertidal zone during the lowest tide windows revealed some of the ways in which the ancestral peoples of the island supported such large populations. We found that much of the foreshore has evidence of complex marine systems in the form of highly engineered stone and wood fish traps and rock-faced terraces used to create clam gardens. On land, there are remnant patches of the highly valued blue camas, which was cultivated throughout the Salish world for its starchy bulb. Patches of crabapple, cultivated for its edible fruit, may also be legacies of ancient plant management systems. These archaeological and ecological features not only reflect highly sophisticated engineering and ecological knowledge, but also the complex governance systems in which this knowledge was enacted.

When viewed through an archaeological lens, the Indigenous history of Xwe'etay is evident almost anywhere you look. Whether it be an impressive coastal village site or an isolated projectile point found on the top of the highest point on the island, the history of Indigenous people is everywhere. We need only open our eyes to a different way of knowing and honouring histories.

Dr. Dana Lepofsky is a professor of archaeology at Simon Fraser University. She is a former president of the Society of Ethnobiology, and winner of the Smith Wintemberg Award in 2018.

ATTRIBUTIONS

1 "The Flying Dutchman," *Pacific Yachting (PY)* Dec. 1993 vol. 35 no 12 ISSN 0030-8986

2 "Early Spanish Footprints," *PY* Feb. 2000 vol. 42 no. 2 ISSN 0030-8986

3 "La Perouse, BC's Forgotten Explorer," *PY* Jul. 1994 vol. 36 no. 7 ISSN 0030-8986

4 "Who Shot Estevan Light?" Harbour Publishing Ltd., *Raincoast Chronicles* #19 Jan. 1998 ISBN 1-55017-171-2

5 "Aflame on the Water: The Final Cruise of the Grappler," Harbour Publishing Ltd., *Raincoast Chronicles* #19 ISBN 1-55017-316-2

6 "Captains in Conflict," *PY* Mar. 2003 vol. 45 no. 3 ISBN 0030-8986

7 "The Strange Story of the Pig War," *PY* Apr. 2001 vol. 43 no.4 ISBN 0030-8986

8 "Typhoon Frieda," published as "Thar' She Blows," *PY* Oct. 2003 vol. 45 no. 10 ISBN 0030-8986

9 "Adrift in the Days Before Radio," *PY* 1999 vol. 41 no. 11 ISSN 0030-8986

10 "Rumrunner Memories," *PY* Apr. 2002 vol. 44 no. 4 ISBN 0030-8986

11 "Father of the Vancouver Island Pilot," *PY* Sept. 2000 vol. 42 no. 9 ISBN 0030-8986

12 "The Calamitous Cruise of the Clio," (Published as "The Curious Cruise of the Clio") *PY* Sept. 1997 vol. 39 no. 9 ISSN 0030-8986

14 "The Great Pox," Harbour Publishing Ltd., *Raincoast Chronicles* #17 1996 ISBN 1-55017-142-9

15 "Destination Haida Gwaanas," previously published as "Destination South Moresby" *PY* Nov. 1992 vol. 34 no. 11 ISSN 0030-8986

16 "Cruising in the Land of the Kwakwaka'wakw," published as "Small Boat Among the Kwakiutl" *PY* Dec. 1990 vol. 32 no. 12 ISSN 0030-8986

17 "In the Wake of Captain Vancouver," published as "In Lieu of Louisa," *PY* Jul. 1997 vol. 28 no. 7 ISSN 0030-8986

18 "Small Boat Necessities," published as "Tender Possibilities," *PY* Jun. 1991 vol. 33 no. 6 ISSN 0030-8986

ACKNOWLEDGEMENTS

I would like to thank so many people, most living in my wonderful community on the beautiful island of Xwe'etay (Lasqueti). Chris Ferris read all my articles and stories to me, as my disability prevented me from reading them myself, and helped with editing. Both Sheila Ray and Izzy Harrington were invaluable typists, transcribing the previously published articles from magazines to computer. Faren Wolfe was essential in helping with researching Indigenous names. Adam Enright put his computer expertise to much appreciated use in many ways. Dana Lepofsky, a Xwe'etay resident and professor of archaeology at Simon Fraser University, was an invaluable resource on all things Indigenous and kindly wrote a fascinating article for this book on Xwe'etay (Lasqueti) archaeology. Vici Johnstone, publisher of Caitlin Press, has done a superb job with this book as she did with my last one, *Accidental Eden*, co-authored with Darlene Olesko. Many thanks to Wayne Bright and Jack Barrett for making my house more livable. My life partner, Penny Sadler, has done editing and much, much more for this book. I also thank *Pacific Yachting* and Howard White of Harbour Publishing Ltd. for originally publishing many of these stories. And great thanks and gratitude to the Indigenous ancestors of Xwe'etay for a half century of life on their beautiful island.

About the Author

Douglas L. Hamilton was born in Washington, DC, and received an MA in history from the University of California, Riverside. In the 1970s he moved to Lasqueti Island where he built a shack made of driftwood on an isolated beach. Soon after, he became interested in writing history pieces for magazines, and his stories have appeared in *Pacific Yachting*, *Raincoast Chronicles*, *Canadian West* and *True West*. His book *Sobering Dilemma: A History of Prohibition in British Columbia* was published by Ronsdale Press in 2004. He enjoys doing lapidary work as a hobby and until recently lived for decades on his property on Lasqueti Island with his partner, her harpsichord, cows and chickens. Unfortunately he was diagnosed with Parkinson's disease and now lives in Parksville.